LIQUID ASSETS

LIQUID ASSETS

How to Develop an Enjoyable and Profitable Wine Portfolio

WILLIAM SOKOLIN

MACMILLAN PUBLISHING COMPANY
New York

MACMILLAN PUBLISHING COMPANY
866 Third Avenue, New York, N.Y. 10022
Collier Macmillan Canada, Inc.

Library of Congress Cataloging-in-Publication Data
Sokolin, William.
  Liquid assets.
  Bibliography: p.
  Includes index.
  1. Wine as an investment.   2. Wine industry.
I. Title.
HD9370.5.S65 1987   332.63   86-31284
ISBN 0-02-612300-2

Macmillan books are available at special discounts for bulk purchases for sales promotions, premiums, fund-raising, or educational use. For details, contact:
                    Special Sales Director
                    Macmillan Publishing Company
                    866 Third Avenue
                    New York, N.Y. 10022

10 9 8 7 6 5 4 3 2 1

PRINTED IN THE UNITED STATES OF AMERICA

To Gloria, Dede and David

CONTENTS

ACKNOWLEDGMENTS

In the course of writing this book I relied on the assistance of many individuals for their time, support and insight. First of all, I'd like to thank Abdullah Simon, Robert Mondavi, Michael Broadbent and David Molyneux Berry, unfailing sources of information on Bordeaux wine. For material regarding wine storage and validation, I am indebted to Roger Livdahl, wine appraiser extraordinaire, who gladly detailed the mechanisms of his art and also provided an insider's view of private cellars. George M. Schofield generously shared his statistical research on the appreciation of California wines, without which several of the charts in this book would not have been possible. Jules Epstein and Jim Crystal helped clarify the special problems of insuring wine. Wine consultant Henry L. Keller shed some light on the thicket of problems posed by state liquor laws. Michael Davis of Christie's, Dennis Foley of Butterfield and Butterfield, John Hart of the Chicago Wine Company and Steven Dyer of the the Texas Art Gallery returned innumerable telephone calls and answered a barrage of questions regarding auction proceedings; their candor is much appreciated. Betsy Camp of KCBX in San Luis Obispo offered a valuable perspective on charity wine auctions, while Larry Goldstein of the Arthur Young accounting firm doggedly pursued the tax questions regarding charitable donations of wine (and then outlined his findings in layman's terms). Christopher Collins graciously supplied written comments on Port vintages and was also an expert source for Port prices in England.

For all of the individuals on whose published work I have so heavily leaned, I express my gratitude, especially to Alexis Lichine, Hugh Johnson, Clive Coates and Nicholas Faith.

This book could not have appeared in its final form without the able assistance of Lindley Boegehold, Ken Rivard, Knut Woehnke and my wife, Gloria.

INTRODUCTION

The term "wine investor" falls harshly on the ears of the old-fashioned lover of Bordeaux. "I drink wines—not invest in them," was a common response to my notion of a book on wine investing. A few of my listeners turned smartly on their heels or snapped their heads in a way that suggested I had just tromped on a favored bed of prize tulips.

"Wine *investment*? Oh, I see."

Meaning, I see you're one of those money-grubbing swine who's willing to put a price on anything—love, art, a happy marriage.

Not true, as I hope you'll discover in the course of reading this book. But still, *wine investor*? In the chapters to come I'll have a lot to say about the wine market. Usually I'll talk about wine lovers or even wine buyers, in the same way someone refers to art lovers. Undeniably, some people purchase art solely because it becomes more valuable year after year, just as some people acquire wine for the same reasons. But knowing the price of a Picasso engraving shouldn't negate my appreciation for its beauty, and the knowledge might actually help me do a better job of investing my meager collector's budget. The principle is even more valuable with wine, where worth is often as much the result of reputation and critical agreement among a coterie of wine writers than any "objective" standard. Anyone who purchases a Lafite or a Pétrus in ignorance of their skyrocketing prices ought to have his head or his pocketbook examined.

Wine is to be drunk, enjoyed and shared with friends, right? If we don't often see a link between the lovely bucolic, pastoral image of the vineyard and the marketplace, it's because we're wearing blinders. After all, it seems a bit squalid to invite thoughts of money to sit at the same table with associations of conviviality and friendship. Moreover, self-important wine writers and critics would have us believe that expensive wine is special, that its price is directly pegged to its celestial taste (which they'll be more than happy to describe for us).

Nothing could be further from the truth. Is it taste that makes a person pay $2,000 for a nineteenth-century Latour? Is it taste that prompts

1

an investment gnome to squirrel away two dozen cases of Mouton-Rothschild in eager anticipation of the next market boom? Of course not. Romance, passion and greed also have their roles to play, as the following stories of Mr. Chesterfield and Mr. Botillo, two wine buyers who frequent my shop, illustrate.

A few years ago a middle-aged man in a chesterfield coat entered my Madison Avenue wine shop. A sheaf of wine reviews thick as the twin barrels of a shotgun poked out from under his arm and he immediately fired off a series of questions. What did I think about the 1983 Bordeaux vintage? Was it overpriced? Was it as good as the 1982? Would I guarantee that if he purchased ten cases the price would triple in five years? How much could he expect his wine to appreciate in six months?

I am a wine merchant, not a commodities broker. Before I encourage anyone to buy wine for future appreciation I try to gauge the depth of their knowledge. Wine lovers can't help but recognize fellow travelers. They have the gravitational affinity of satellites revolving around the same planet; they swap stories about visits to vineyards, about the first time they tasted particular favorites, about the liquid treasure they discovered in an offbeat restaurant.

Did Mr. Chesterfield love wine?

Alas, he did not.

Mr. Chesterfield, I quickly discovered, had never purchased more than two bottles of wine at a time. But his friends, several of whom had cellars, had regaled him with tales of the extraordinary 1982 vintage, how prices for red Bordeaux wines had doubled and even tripled before the wines were even released from the châteaux. Although he assumed that his friends were alcoholic madmen, he had nevertheless researched the wines in several magazines and newsletters. Now, satisfied that he had discovered the pot of gold at the end of the rainbow, he was grilling me for the exact details on just what sort of return he could expect on his money.

Perhaps, I suggested as gently as I could, he wasn't the sort of person who was suited to wine investing.

Mr. Chesterfield brushed my advice aside. That afternoon he purchased $5,000 worth of first-growth red Bordeaux. He didn't even take delivery. At that time I had a policy of offering a year's free storage for any order of ten cases or more. Every week for the next two years, Mr. Chesterfield telephoned me. How much were his wines worth? What happened to the market surge of the year before? Why wasn't he doubling his money? After twenty-four months of watching his investment appreciate agonizingly slowly, he sold the entire lot at auction. The wines were in immaculate condition—they had never been touched, not even by Mr. Chesterfield. After auction fees, his return was a Scrooge-like nine percent, hardly the sort of dizzying gain that inspires potential investors to scramble for their checkbooks. Mr. Chesterfield's soul, if he had one, would have been as satisfied to sit down with a glass containing a municipal bond as one filled with Château Margaux.

Mr. Botillo, a retired investment banker who grew up in the Bronx, represents a different sort of client altogether. He loves serving famous old wines at his dinner parties. His name was at the top of my list for people to call when I came into possession of a "library" of rare nineteenth-century wines.

1870 Lafite? Wonderful!

1847 Château Rauzan? Can't wait to taste it!

1867 Mouton-Rothschild? A steal! How can I fight a bargain at $1,500 a bottle!

These wines sell for prices that would make the blood drain from other clients' faces, yet for Mr. Botillo the chance to taste wines that were around when Lincoln signed the Emancipation Proclamation, that graced tables in the England of Queen Victoria and Disraeli—this experience was almost beyond value. My banker friend's only stipulation was that whatever I offered him had to be available in lots of at least four bottles. He couldn't stand the thought of inviting someone for dinner and then running out of a particular vintage. Wine, as a commodity that appreciates in value, wasn't of the remotest concern to him. But wines that had danced with history, how could you calculate their worth?

Every writer tries to conjure up his imaginary audience. After all, who wants to project his words into a void? My audience is a blend of the Chesterfield and Botillo in everyone. In practical terms, this book is an answer to the questions posed by the wine-loving community embodied in my friends and clients. Some are rich, some are scrupulously thrifty, but most of them are interested in mixing their pleasure with profit. Even my very wealthy clients gasped at the rapid price escalation of the 1982 Bordeaux wines. What was going on? If you're considering making your first case purchase of wine, then you should be concerned as well. The following chapters should help you cross the psychological gulf that separates those who measure their purchases in cases from those who buy one bottle at a time. Though ultimately the total quantity of wine consumed may be the same, the man or woman with a liquid investment beneath his feet holds different opinions about his wine than one whose view extends only as far as what's standing on the kitchen counter for tonight's dinner party. At the very least, the man with a cellar, after a few years, drinks his wines for free.

Are you like Mr. Chesterfield, hoping to make a quick killing in French châteaux? Or more like Mr. Botillo, enraptured with wine's history and associations?

Ideally, you're a little of both. This book will not make you rich. But it will show you how to benefit from the changes coming to the wine market. Right now the wine trade and the wine consumer are in a period of rapid transition. A historic jump in prices over the last ten years has made it foolhardy—unless you have unlimited wealth—to acquire certain wines, primarily first-growth red Bordeaux, without considering their investment potential. Quite possibly other wines will follow suit. Moreover, state laws are beginning to favor the consumer. Presently there are two states that permit the direct resale of wine by private individuals—California and Illinois. New York State is about to permit this type of transaction; more will follow in the next few years. Those who anticipate these changes will reap mightily as states liberalize their laws.

The principles of wine investment are not difficult. The most crucial of them pertain to recognizing investment wine and then knowing how to sell it. Although all investment-grade wine usually has a time in its life span when most wine lovers collectively assert its ambrosial flavor, taste alone is a poor guide for investment. In addition to discussing the salient features of investment-grade wine, I will provide a quick introduction to specific wines with investment value, and the vineyards that produce them.

Wine has rewarded my family well. I've spent over half my life in the wine business, gathering a host of precious family experiences connected with wine. My wife and I honeymooned in Burgundy. I introduced Château Gloria to this country because Gloria is my wife's name. My son and daughter—then two and seven—cooed with pleasure when we first fed each of them a spoon of Cantemerle (after having soundly rejected, at separate tastings, the wines of a dozen other châteaux). My mother, who had no formal knowledge of wine, was always a great intuitive judge of a wine's taste. How many stories and how many bottles we've shared with our loved ones! *Liquid Assets* is an invitation to introduce the same principles of profit and pleasure into your own life.

CHAPTER ONE

WINE INVESTING CROSSES THE ATLANTIC

Speculation is so much more fun than marketing that the [wine] trade is still addicted to it.

—NICHOLAS FAITH

Our perceptions about how and why we buy wine are undergoing a sea change. Once the distant uncle of the liquor business, hoary with the traditions and trappings of snobbery, the wine trade has undergone a transformation in the last two decades. At the heart of this evolution is the passage of certain wines from genteel beverages into investment collectibles.

Americans, newly introduced to the investment side of wine, are often shocked at the increase in prices for the very best French wines, especially in the last fifteen years. Talcum powder, Swiss cheese and wool overcoats haven't risen by a factor of ten, and the price of caviar has actually decreased of late, so why should wine increase by leaps and bounds? To think of wine as an object whose value can rise because of market speculation or a suddenly fashionable desire to be "in wine" seems unsavory.

Fine wine, like collectibles, has always had an air of speculation about it. The history of making and selling wine in modern times is a history of gambling. Wine prices are easily as volatile as those of art, perhaps more so. If this unsuspected aspect of fine wine has only come to our attention recently, it's probably because, as Americans, we're the Johnny-come-latelies of the wine market. Europeans, with their long historical and cultural involvement with wine, are more attuned to the economic vicissitudes of making and selling wine, and thus more accustomed to radical price shifts.

Like any business, the trade has enjoyed its share of unscrupulous speculators and confidence men, merchants who imported the produce of Algerian vineyards as "claret," and undisciplined growers more inter-

5

ested in squeezing the maximum tonnage out of each vineyard hectare than in making great wine. It is also a business filled with dedicated people who produce and market a great product in the face of ruin. Wine's elegant image, its connotations of pastoral serenity, isn't inaccurate as much as incomplete.

In the early chapters of his wonderful book, *The Winemasters*, Nicholas Faith provides an amusing and cogent history of the Bordeaux wine trade, especially the relationship between merchants and growers. However, beneath the surface of his narrative runs a current of risk and despair, of men desperately clinging to their livelihood, hoping somehow that next year will redeem present misfortunes. Growers and merchants have never had it easy, although growers seem to have had it worse. The Bordeaux merchants, often emigrating from England, Ireland and other parts of Europe, traded on their foreign origins, providing a vital market otherwise beyond the reach of growers. Merchants also supplied the capital necessary to sustain growers through periods of bad weather and disease. The merchants expected high compensation for their investment, often in the form of merciless *abonnements*, contracts obligating a grower to sell his vineyard's output to a merchant for a set term of years (usually five or ten) at a set price. *Abonnements* have sometimes saved growers, but just as often they've insulated them from the beneficial effects of a booming wine market. Growers have often stood helpless, watching merchants grow rich as foreign markets began bidding up the price for a successful vintage. Merchants, too, have had their share of risks. Uncertain relations between London and Paris and the political turmoil of eighteenth-century France often interrupted their business. Cargoes could be lost at sea, and the sheer capital-intensive nature of winemaking made the trade a risky business. A string of bad years might affect growers first, but the merchants were never completely immune. Nicholas Faith's account is strewn with the specters of bankrupt vintners and merchants alike.

Is it any wonder, with the potential for ruin so close at hand, that when an opportunity to raise prices presented itself, growers and merchants often obliged? Faith also offers stories of legendary financial coups in the Bordeaux wine market, especially attempts to corner all or part of the market—Herman Cruse's virtual monopoly of the 1847 vintage, Edouard Kressman's similar role in the vintage of 1870 and, in more recent times, the huge purchases of the 1959 vintage by Jean-Pierre Mouiex (of Château Pétrus fame). Gamblers? Speculators? Or simply good businessmen with a keen eye on market conditions? The buying and selling of wine has been notoriously subject to seasonal changes— in the weather and in fashion. Far more so than the items whose price stability we would like wine to emulate. The business survives by the efforts of men willing to gamble.

IN THE BEGINNING THERE WAS ENGLAND

Although sales of wine in England have been recorded for the last three centuries, the establishment of the great private cellars reaches back hardly two hundred years and the popularization of wine among the middle classes dates only from the time of Dickens. Bordeaux wines of quality, specifically the upper register of red wines, were a province of the wealthy, the only people (then, as now) who could afford them. Wealthy English cellared their wines so as to be able to drink them, not as a hedge against inflation or with thoughts of their profitable resale. But the roots of our present investment approach to wine can still be found on eighteenth-century auction blocks, as wine becomes available to private individuals for the highest bid. The list of items offered at Christie's very first auction, in 1766, mentions "Genuine Household Furniture, Jewels, Fire-Arms, etc. and a large Quantity of Madeira and high Flavour'd Claret, late the Property of a Noble Personage (Deceas'd)." Christie's, as well as other auctioneers, has sold wine intermittently up to the present day.

Edmund Penning-Rowsell, the venerable British wine writer, devoted a short article in a 1986 Christie's catalogue to the history of the firm's wine auctions. Unlike the spirited movement of wine of the present day, he recalls that until the Second World War wine auctions "were largely conducted for private clients, whose death or removal had led to the private dispersal of their cellars." This dour picture took on an even grayer cast during the fifties. Christie's wine auction rooms had been bombed and as a consequence the firm didn't resume auctioning wine until 1953. The devastating frost of 1956 struck a terrible blow at Bordeaux, necessitating several years of recovery before France could even offer a reasonable product for sale. Wine departments within the major auction houses, organized along the same lines as, say, a department devoted exclusively to ceramics or silver, date from the very recent past. A decade of price increases, including the boosts of 1959 and 1961, as well as a growing international clientele with fine wine to sell, prompted auctioneers to take this next step. Michael Broadbent founded the wine department at Christie's in 1966; Sotheby's, lagging slightly behind, formed their own wine department in 1970.

In the sixties, England liberalized the laws regarding wine sales, a change that coincided with (and contributed to) the rapid expansion of a market for wine. Penning-Rowsell notes that whereas the average Englishman drank only two and half bottles of wine in 1960, he managed to wade into a dozen bottles annually fifteen years later. Wine, and this is important because it mirrors a similar change in the United States, was acquiring a popular acceptance. As inexpensive versions of a product become popular, and people educate themselves in its appreciation, then the demand for even finer versions of the item increases. That such a demand would increase the fine wine market is clear, especially as the association of better wine exclusively with the upper classes begins to erode. If you can afford it, buy it.

In present-day England there exists a very active investment market in fine and rare wine. Sotheby's, Phillips and Christie's, the largest auction houses, continue to maintain and expand their wine departments. In 1985, Christie's alone sold over $10 million in international wine auctions, with over half of that figure deriving from auctions in its St. James offices alone.

Nor does the English investment market depend exclusively on the auction houses. When it seemed as though London risked losing its market share in the fine wine trade some years ago, the government sanctioned a plan of tax incentives to encourage investment in the wine trade. Though recently discontinued, the arrangement, known as the BES, for Business Expansion Scheme, allowed private investors to purchase shares in wine-trading groups, as long as they agreed to maintain the investment for at least five years. Private individuals also have the option of trading with smaller firms like Collins, or Corney and Barrows, who offer a variety of services such as storing wine stocks for individuals, as well as buying and selling wine on the auction market and through private sale.

I do not want to leave you with the impression that Great Britain alone allows its citizens to invest freely in wine. In greater or lesser degrees, depending on the type of transaction and the particular countries involved, such opportunities also exist for continental Europeans. Only in America is this investment avenue curtailed—but not completely—and that, as we shall see, is changing.

THE AMERICAN MARKET
GETTING STARTED—THE SIXTIES

In the early sixties an enthusiastic wine lover purchased a few cases of 1961 Château Pétrus and 1961 Mouton-Rothschild from me for what then seemed like the phenomenally high prices of $120 and $250 per case. An English firm recently purchased his remaining two cases of Pétrus for $10,000 each. He has since been offered $5,000 for each remaining case of Mouton. Selling the wine didn't enter his mind when he made his purchase. Like many of my early clients, he was part of a growing cadre of wine lovers who, starting in the fifties, began to make the American appetite for fine wine a major force in the Bordeaux and Burgundy market.

Between 1970 and 1984 the average prices for first-growth red Bordeaux skyrocketed almost *fifteen hundred percent.* While increased taxes, higher prices for cork, glass bottles and escalating production costs account for a hefty chunk of wine's higher price, the fact remains that luxury wines have a much broader market now than they did a few short years ago. As Americans we have changed our drinking habits, our perceptions about wine and how we spend our money on alcoholic beverages. All of these have contributed to the present boom in wine, and by extension, the value and importance of wine as an investment. My client, who bought his wines at the beginning of the boom, now looks to have gotten quite a bargain, and the sales of just a few of his early purchase will finance most of his future wine expenses.

As a wine retailer and importer for the past thirty years I've had a ringside seat for the changing spectacle of America's involvement in wine. In many respects, my own evolution as a lover and buyer of wines has paralleled that of the country as a whole. Viewed from the perspective of a liquor merchant, the America of 1960 was an altogether different country from the America of 1986. In 1960 we were a nation in love with hard liquor and mixed drinks. Among the hordes of two-fisted martini and scotch aficionados I rarely encountered a man or woman who knew wines at all, let alone well. Aside from the occasional sommelier, the client who showed some familiarity with wine often came from the sort of monied class I associated with Thurber cartoons, or had spent time in France. My father had never sold much wine in his liquor business because there wasn't a market for it.

But in 1960 an event occurred which turned my perspective upside down. After a long illness, my father died in 1959. I operated his liquor business for a year after his death, unable to decide whether to sell out or commit myself to it. Then Dreyfus and Ashby, a British firm with connections to the Portuguese wine trade, offered me exclusive rights to an unknown rosé they thought might be popular. The name of the rosé was Mateus. What decided me was seeing Ray Milland in a movie that had just come out. My eyes jumped to the screen—a bottle of Mateus was sitting on his table! I concluded that Mateus must be pretty sophisticated stuff if a character with Ray Milland's breeding and charm was drinking it. Cases of funny green bottles arrived at my shop and soon people were calling my store from all over New York just for a bottle of rosé. The devotion of a clientele to an odd green bottle filled with pink wine astonished me. Who were these people? What else did they drink? Could there be a wine market out there? Had I leaned over the side of the Staten Island Ferry and glimpsed the turrets of a submerged city, perfectly preserved on the bottom of New York harbor, I wouldn't have been more surprised.

Several months later I still couldn't quite believe the evidence so I decided to test the waters again. This time I ordered twenty-five cases of a private-label Châteauneuf-du-Pape from Dreyfus and Ashby (mean-

ing I would be listed as the importer on the bottle). Twenty-five cases!
Twenty-five cases will easily fit inside a couple of telephone booths, but
in my imagination I thought they would fill a warehouse. Liquor stores
did not typically have extensive wine selections then, and when they
did, they were a modest array of French wines. Few people had ever
heard of Rhone wines, and California might as well have been on
another planet. Shortly after the wine arrived I heard Jack Paar mention on his television show that he liked wine. The next day, after an
unsuccessful attempt to reach him on the telephone, I wrote a letter
describing the du-Pape. He bought the first five cases; the rest sold
in a matter of months. The sale made me a believer. In the following three decades I would introduce over a dozen new wines to the
New York market, but none gave me quite the thrill of the Mateus
and Châteauneuf-du-Pape. They were the prophets, announcing that
America, popular America, was becoming wine country.

My recollections of the decade after 1960 are of a mad scramble for
education, an attempt to educate myself about wine and an effort to
educate wine clients. Newspapers began featuring the comments of wine
writers. Trade people interested in fostering a greater public knowledge
of wine began giving public lectures. Harold Grossman spread the word
through his famous wine-tasting classes at the Waldorf-Astoria. Within
months of my experience with Châteauneuf du-Pape I read everything
I could find on Beaujolais (not a lengthy task) and then invited people
to my apartment on East Thirty-fifth Street for Wednesday evening
tastings and discussion of Beaujolais. In those days a firsthand education
in French wines cost relatively little, since everything except the very
top-flight wines was modestly priced.

During this period I'd do anything to make people aware of wine.
William F. Buckley's *National Review* had its offices on the floor directly
above my apartment. After everyone had left, I'd slip my brief catalogue of wines under the door of the *Review*. At my athletic club, members would return from a round of handball and find catalogues in their
lockers. I passed on tips from my Waldorf-Astoria class to my Wednesday evening groups: always taste wines as you're reading about them.
Fortunately for me, no one followed it too closely; considering the small
number of books on wine, if they had taken my advice seriously my
fledgling career as a wine merchant would have ground to a dead halt.

I tasted enough wine during those early years to discover that a
great wine always remains a mysterious, elusive commodity, a possession whose final appeal is not subject to analysis. Any luxury item depends on this. The day black truffles and golden caviar appear on the
grocery shelves next to macaroni and cheese is the day they lose their
allure. They would still taste just as delicious, but their essential mystique would be gone. An education in the subtleties the best vineyards
have to offer us should demystify, yet leave the mystique intact.

BOOM TIMES: THE SEVENTIES

The seventies were a breakthrough decade because people began to ac-knowledge the appeal of wine without sacrificing its cachet. This de-cade also gave Americans their first taste of a wine boom rapidly followed by a market collapse. In the first years of the seventies prices for first-growths doubled, while the less-well-known wines of the 1855 Médoc classification tended to climb at a slower pace.

About this time I got the notion that fine wine was money. Terry Robards, the wine critic for the *New York Times,* was good enough to print my views in a Sunday column. Enough people were impressed with the idea—hardly news to the French and English, but novel enough on this side of the Atlantic—that a few investor magazines solicited my ideas and I suddenly found myself asked to speak on radio talk shows about wine investment. I ran an advertisement in the *Times,* offering to appraise the investment value of private cellars. For the second time in my wine career I was astonished: my shop received over two hundred inquiries concerning private collections, ranging in size from $4,000 to $5,000 on up to a physician with almost $10 million worth of old wines stored in the hillside cellar behind his house.

A few investment bankers were beginning to act on my ideas. They bought various amounts of classified Grands Crus (the "great growths" of the Médoc region in Bordeaux). A wealthy Iranian, with no wine knowledge at all, bought over $1 million of Bordeaux vintages as well. I don't claim to have started the gold rush for expensive wine in the early seventies, but I certainly helped it along. In the first months of 1973 prices escalated wildly (or what I thought was wildly, until the early eighties showed me the real meaning of the word). All investment experts will agree that no market can sustain a price surge indefinitely; if this were not the case, all we'd have to do is invest our money, sit back and watch our dollars multiply. Where the experts begin to break ranks is over the anticipated arrival of the break in prices. In April of 1973 the balloon began to lose its air. The Iranian, furious to see a slight downturn in prices, dumped his wine on the market, helping to precipitate a further drop in prices. Panic selling drove the market into a downward spiral. I vividly remember a case of 1961 Pétrus fetching $1,500 in April. A few months later the case was available for less than half that price. The market took until 1978 to recover, and then began another cycle upward. The year 1961 Pétrus, by the way, sold for $12,000 in 1986, providing a salutary lesson to those who think that the wine market is easy game for quick-kill artists.

The blaze of speculative fervor of the early seventies proved to be a candle compared to the bonfire of activity that has characterized the eighties. Prices for the 1982 Bordeaux vintage opened high and began to jump as soon as enraptured wine writers like Robert Parker, Jr., be-

gan mailing back their tasting notes from France. Prices doubled, and
in the case of Pétrus, tripled, after only eighteen months of the first
futures offering; older vintages of the same wines increased in value
proportionately. As word spread from wine lover to wine lover, a buying frenzy seized the trade, fueling further price increases. For the first
time since becoming involved in the wine business I advised clients to
approach their purchases cautiously. In my opinion these wines weren't
worth their staggering prices; certainly, it seemed foolish to spend this
much money for an unproven wine that hadn't even been shipped to
the United States yet.

Some people, unintentionally, have realized extraordinary profits
during the present boom market simply by having purchased investment-grade wine years ago and then reselling after 1982. A Brazilian
friend of mine called Herman wanted to open a first-class French restaurant in New York in 1965. A colorful, well-traveled man, Herman
had visited the top-flight restaurants of Europe. He was determined that
his own establishment would feature a good wine list. The first table
below shows his original purchases, accompanied by the cost per case
in 1965, and what he would have paid had he attempted to finance the
same list in 1985. All cases are for twelve 750 ml bottles, unless otherwise indicated.

QUANTITY	WINE	PRICE/CASE (1965)	PRICE/CASE (1986)
10 cases	1959 Lafite	$162	$4,800
10 cases	1961 Mouton-Rothschild	188	5,000
10 cases	1962 Pétrus	120	5,000
10 cases	1964 Lafite	66	2,400
10 cases	1964 Lynch-Bages	31	750
10 cases	1953 Margaux	195	4,500
10 cases	1955 Calon-Ségur	68	1,450
10 cases	1955 Montrose	59	1,500
10 cases	1959 La Mission-Haut-Brion	78	3,600
10 cases	1961 Palmer	140	5,000
(various bottles)			
100 cases	1962 La Lagune	28	600
(the house bar wine)			
3 cases	1961 Romanée-Conti	200	6,500

The capital expenditure to establish such a wine list in 1965 was
obviously a fraction of its cost two decades later. Herman continued
purchasing wines from me. In the late seventies he sold the restaurant,
but kept the wine cellar. The list below shows what remained when he
liquidated the cellar in 1985. Some of the wines were purchased as late
as 1974.

QUANTITY	WINE	PRICE/CASE (PURCHASE)	PRICE/CASE (SALE)
3 cases	1959 Lafite	$162	$4,000
3 cases (magnums)	1959 Lafite	162	4,000
2 cases (magnums)	1967 Lafite	50	690
15 cases	1964 Lafite	56	2,000
10 cases	1966 Latour	90	2,300
3 cases	1966 Pétrus	110	5,000
12 cases	1966 Margaux	78	2,100
5 cases (magnums)	1970 Trotanoy	56	780
1 case (magnums)	1970 Pichon-Lalande	70	750

Herman didn't buy these wines as investments. However, being in the right place at the right time paid off handsomely for him. The soaring price differences are truly remarkable, but not unusual for anyone who happened to purchase wines before the present boom got into full swing. With price increases as radical as these it's difficult to see how anyone can regard the market for fine wine as anything *but* investment.

Each year we buy more and more investment-grade wines (even at present prices). A recent article in the *Wine Spectator* examined the American and British markets for red Bordeaux wines in the first four years of this decade. While the markets had grown on both sides of the Atlantic, the *value* of the American purchases had risen at an astounding rate of almost thirty percent annually. We're buying more wines; more importantly, we're buying more expensive wines, further proof of our investment orientation toward the fine wine market.

Another factor to examine is the annual rate of appreciation for investment-grade French and California wines, almost twenty percent for California, slightly higher for wines from France. Most investors I know would be delighted to average twenty percent on their money annually. The number of telephone calls I receive from people monitoring the prices of upper-tier Bordeaux wines suggests that they have an interest in their cellars that extends beyond considerations of aesthetics.

In recent years an extensive underground market for wines has developed. Consultants, brokers and others in the trade disagree on its size, but the mere fact that so many collectors have admitted to knowing of transactions suggests to me that it's sizable. Advertisements soliciting buyers for private cellars appear regularly in various wine periodicals.

Many collectors, perhaps most of them, would rather sell their wine on the open market, but the tangle of differing state regulations, the aftermath of Prohibition, proves so daunting that they find it more convenient to operate on the "quiet market."

Massive purchases of wine by individuals not involved in the wine trade is another telltale sign of investment interest. In September of 1986 one of New York's oldest, most established merchants sold all his remaining 1985 futures for first-growth red Bordeaux—to a single individual. I contacted the buyer, who refused to tell me the size of the transaction, but at the very least it involved several hundred thousand dollars and hundreds of cases of wine. Obviously the buyer doesn't intend to drink his wine; he anticipates selling it, presumably by 1990. Quite possibly this investor intends to liquidate his holdings through one of the several legal avenues open to him. But equally possible is that he's already noticed the changing legal climate regarding wine's resale. With certain restrictions, it's already legal to sell your wine at any of the various national auctions sponsored by charities or firms like Christie's or Butterfield and Butterfield. And California, pioneer in so many areas of the wine trade, has enacted a ground-breaking piece of legislation: private individuals, since January of 1986, have been able to sell their back wines to retailers. The law is not perfect, but it takes us one step closer to the sort of unfettered market now seen in Europe. Similar legislation has come up for the last three years in New York State. I believe that the next decade will see one state after another allowing private citizens to engage in the direct resale of their wine.

WHERE WE'RE GOING

Wine investing is an idea whose time has come, not as another scheme that promises us the opportunity to trade our Fords for Ferraris, but to enhance the original purpose of wine—to bring pleasure at an affordable price. Those who sneer at the idea of investing in wine would do well to take an example from the English upper classes—wine investing is the least expensive way of financing a cellar. I've pointed out some of the more obvious signs of the investment potential in wine in order to demonstrate that wine has another aspect deserving your time and thought. Wine investing is the conscious planning for what you'll be drinking in the future. With a little luck that should be considerably better than what you can afford to drink now. In 1960 I treated Mateus like Lafite. I didn't know any better. Look at this book primarily as a simple set of suggestions about the world's most charming pastime, the appreciation of wine. Along the path to the vineyards you'll see how to leaven your pleasure—with profit.

CHAPTER TWO

DISCOVERING INVESTMENT-GRADE WINE

Picking investment-grade wine (or IGW, as I like to call it) is a lot like picking stocks. In both cases you're looking for an item that will provide you with a high rate of return, and you're making your selection from an enormous field of possible alternatives. In retrospect, the stocks whose prices have risen or which have paid dividends in the course of a year usually exhibit a set of distinctive features—sound management, an innovative marketing strategy or a research breakthrough. With some practice you can learn to identify those characteristics which bode well (or ill) for a company's future; you buy and sell accordingly.

Identifying investment-grade wine means learning to recognize wines which will make money. Like stocks which perform well, IGW has qualities which set it apart from other wines; chief among these are longevity and public recognition. First of all, wine which measures its life span in decades, rather than months, improves in flavor as it ages, increasing its value to those who appreciate its complexity of taste; secondly, a wine with a lifetime of thirty or fifty or one hundred years may be traded without fear of spoilage.

Public recognition also contributes to the value of a wine, though perhaps in a less quantifiable manner. History, myth and passion always provoke our interest; given two wines of identical quality and price, the force of one wine's reputation, the measure of its esteem among connoisseurs and the strength of the image it evokes in the public's mind will always tip the scales in its favor. In short, the wine with a reputation will eventually cost more.

If you're a wine lover who finds investment appealing, then it's important to understand the variables in the production of fine wine. You can safely assume that all IGW is fine wine, but most fine wine is rarely IGW. Understanding the dynamics of this relationship is the subject of this chapter.

FACTORS IN THE DEVELOPMENT OF FINE WINE

Oenologists (scientists who study wine) and most wine writers generally attribute a wine's quality to five or six variables, some of which may be changed at the winemaker's will, others lying beyond his influence. In brief, these variables are:

- Soil
- Geology
- Weather
- Choice of grape
- Air Quality
- Vinification (the techniques used to make the wine)

The composition of a vineyard's soil has a direct bearing on the quality of the grapes it will produce, and ultimately its wine. The root system of the vine absorbs minerals and nutrients which flavor the grapes. The age of a vineyard and the particular practices of the winemaker contribute to the quality of the soil. A thick layer of rich topsoil in an older vineyard is often the result of years of enrichment (manuring or plowing clover or vine prunings into the dirt between the vines). In Burgundy, the famous topsoil of the Domaine de la Romanée-Conti was imported by the cartload from surrounding environs, a practice condoned in the eighteenth century, but strictly forbidden today. The right soil, as evidenced in Burgundy, Napa and Sonoma, combined with intensive pruning, is a significant factor in producing intensely flavored grapes. The defects of soil can also make themselves known in the grapes. Soils with an excessive iron content, for example, can pass that metallic taste onto the grapes, and eventually the wine.

Poor topsoil need not be an insurmountable obstacle. Scientific opinion seems to be shifting greater importance to a different aspect of vineyard earth, its geology—how the various layers of subsoil and rock strata affect drainage and root growth. For centuries one of the paradoxes of winemaking was that great wines often seemed to come from vineyards where the soil and weather seemed least hospitable to vines. We now know that poor topsoil encourages vines to send down deep roots; the older the vine, the deeper the roots. Subsoils, in the form of gravel, limestone, clay and sand, vary in their ability to retain water and heat, thereby inhibiting or encouraging the growth of the roots.

Hugh Johnson, the famous wine writer and vineyard cartographer, in his *World Atlas of Wine* cites a study by Dr. Gérard Seguin of the University of Bordeaux, confirming a correlation between the quality of a vineyard's drainage and its classification. Not surprisingly, the first-growths had the best drainage; the second-growths came next; the thirds followed the seconds; and so on.

One day, after lunching with Alexis Lichine at his Château Prieuré-Lichine, I walked with him through his vineyard. From time to time he paused, waving his stick at the ground. Dark slate outcroppings broke through the ground around the vines. Such extrusions, he explained, provided the best drainage for nearby vines; these vines produced his best grapes and consequently his finest wine.

I asked him what single factor most determined whether a wine would be great or merely adequate.

Without hesitating he tapped the ground with his stick. "Young man, know your slate."

The optimum climate for vines is not necessarily the best climate for wine grapes. Hugh Johnson observes that the best wines tend to come from vineyards located right on the edge of a climatic zone, the place where a vine has to struggle. This is because the grower's intention is twofold: he wants to produce grapes, but to make wine they must be intensely flavored. Hence, while a minimum of sunlight and rain are critical, too much of either can ruin a vintage. Cabernet Sauvignon vines yield much more fruit in a warm Mediterranean climate than in Bordeaux, but wines made from these grapes taste insipid and thin, as though the vine, able to produce only so much fruit flavor, had to distribute it over twice as many grapes.

The timing of sunshine, rainfall and frost can also ruin or enhance a vintage. A severe frost coming on top of the flowering of the vines will damage or destroy the vulnerable buds destined to turn into grapes, nipping a vintage before it's even been born. Late rains can swell the grapes before harvest, seriously diluting their flavor.

Different grape varieties produce different wines, and depending on the technique and skill of the winemaker, the same grape may produce a light, fruity wine intended for immediate consumption, or it may yield a dark, tannic beverage unfit for drinking until at least a decade has passed. Grapes and root stock also differ according to their yield and their resistance to the Pandora's box of mildew, rot, bacteria and pests that plague vineyards. Different combinations of soil, geology and climate produce a variety of responses in the same strain of grape. Cabernet Sauvignon, one of the three principal grapes used to make red wines in Bordeaux, has a tendency to ripen too quickly under the hot California sun; in Bordeaux, the grape takes weeks longer to reach maturity, making late September a suspense-filled time when growers anxiously keep one eye on their ripening grapes and the other on the autumnal sky, dreading the late rains which can ruin a vintage.

In France a complicated system of laws regulates which grapes may be used to make the fine wines of a given geographic region. The laws are a codification of several centuries of winemaking experience. But in California (or Australia or Argentina or anywhere, for that matter, where new vineyards spring up) the greatest challenge when starting a new vineyard is matching the grapes and root stock to the particularities of the local terrain and climate. California Cabernets have proven themselves to be worthy competitors to their French equivalents, even if the wines are not identical in style. Pinot Noir, the grape used most often in the making of red wines from Burgundy, has been less successful.

Wine lovers who understand the relationship among soil, geology, climate and the different grape varieties are in a better position to select wines from an uneven vintage than those who do not. Take one example. A frost in the spring of 1984 wiped out much of the early-budding Merlot grapes. Since red wines in Bordeaux are blends of various percentages of Merlot, Cabernet Sauvignon, Cabernet Franc and Petit Verdot, the wines that did best in 1984 (not a great year for anybody) came from regions like Margaux, where winemakers depended less heavily on Merlot. Pomerol and St.-Émilion, on the other hand, whose estates rely heavily or predominantly on Merlot, suffered the most.

The quality of air near a vineyard is not often mentioned as a serious factor affecting the quality of wine. It should be. In the late sixties and early seventies, several large oil refineries and pollution-generating industries began operating in and around the Médoc and Graves regions of Bordeaux. At the time, this area produced eighty to ninety percent of the world's most famous wines. The Shell Oil Company, for one, vastly increased its refinery adjacent to the Lafite vineyards. Although Shell publicly guaranteed the cleanliness of its operation, their shooting fires marred the vineyard landscape each night, and I found the affected wines to be somewhat fickle in taste. The price of wines from the areas outside the Médoc and Graves achieved a temporary boost—not by reason of an improvement in grower reliability, drainage or climate, but by fears that vineyards nearest the refinery would be tainted. In the end, we decided that pollution was not a factor.

WINEMAKER EXPERTISE

The human variable in winemaking enters in the person of the winemaker. In the previous section I omitted a discussion of vinification because the sum total of an estate's or winery's ability to benefit from a choice selection of land, climate and fruit resides in the talent of its winemaker (or oenologist, if he or she has undergone formal training). In a narrow sense, vinification refers exclusively to the process of transforming the newly harvested grapes into wine; in the broader view it pertains to the whole range of activity which comes under the winemaker's mantle. This may include decisions regarding which vines are old and need replacing, whether or not to fertilize or manure, when and what to spray for which pests, and perhaps the most important decision of the entire year—when to pick the grapes.

One measure of a grower's astuteness is his ability to judge the precise moment the grapes should be picked, the moment the grapes reach exactly the right levels of acidity and sweetness. The 1969 Brane-Cantenac, for example, stands out in my mind as a fine wine in an otherwise dismal vintage. The grower picked the grapes at the perfect time. Conversely, it's quite possible to reduce an excellent crop of grapes into a poor vintage simply by picking them too early or too late.

All of this precedes the actual process of vinifying the grapes; depending on the quality of the desired wine, the size of the estate and its position in the hierarchy of vineyards, the actual steps of vinification may be strictly prescribed by law or left (within broad limits) to the winemaker's discretion.

In either event, the winemaker translates the vintage from raw fruit into alcoholic beverage. His guidance determines whether the wine will be "fine," merely good or mediocre. A good winemaker, with the aid of modern technology, can save a poor vintage from catastrophe and elevate a vintage into a historic wine.

Great winemakers, most of whom remain unknown to the majority of wine lovers, are the bulwark of fine wine production. The value of the services of an Andre Tchelistcheff at Beaulieu Vineyards or a Jean-Pierre Mouiex at Château Pétrus are beyond estimation. Mouiex has made Pétrus the single most sought after wine in the world; Tchelistcheff introduced oak barrels into California and his Georges de Latour Private Reserve Cabernet showed the world that Americans were capable of making wine the equal of any from France.

Winemakers, as we shall see, exert a profound influence over whether a wine develops investment potential. During vinification the winemaker, depending on his skill, makes several decisions that affect the longevity (and by extension the investment potential) of the wine. Oenologists may also actively become involved in the promotion of the wine, another critical step if the wine is to appreciate in value.

Proprietors have been known to consult independent oenologists, especially if the estate is too small to support a full-time winemaker, or if the proprietor is dissatisfied with the performance of his wines in previous vintages. Professor Emile Peynaud, formerly head of the Station Oenologique at the University of Bordeaux, has a list of past clients that reads like a Who's Who of Bordeaux's famous vineyards—Lafite, Margaux, Cheval Blanc, Ducru-Beaucaillou and Léoville-Lascases, among others.

Professor Peynaud, certainly France's most famous oenologist, may also be its most influential. Under his direct guidance (and the guidance of his former students) Peynaud has flattened some the stylistic hills and gullies which previously helped to set one vineyard apart from its neighbors in Bordeaux. As a demanding consultant, he often pushes his lesser-known clients into producing the elegant, refined style of wine made famous by the first-growths (and the sort of style traditionally associated with IGW). Peynaud's approach is sometimes faulted; his name is mentioned in connection with the attempts by many *petits châteaux* to imitate the style of the great estates, often at the expense of a rustic charm previously associated with wines from smaller vineyards. Certainly Peynaud wines tend to become more expensive. He advocates a rigorous selection process, carefully deciding which grapes will go into the estate's "first wine" (the one with the château name on the bottle), and which will go for a "second wine."

For better or worse, Professor Peynaud has done much to establish the dominant style for expensive red Bordeaux, and evidence of his work in a vineyard is always a sign that the proprietor has committed himself to making wines that are elegant and refined.

Generally speaking, a vineyard with a "hot" winemaker, especially in California, should be examined closely. A winemaker with a string of fine wines to his credit is the best place to find a baby IGW.

ASPECTS OF IGW

PRICE HISTORY. The degree to which a wine's price increases over time determines its suitability as an investment. If a wine doesn't make money, then it's not IGW. A bottle of wine that retails for $5 in 1980 and is resold for $100 in 1990 is investment grade. A delicious wine that costs $45 in 1980 and $50 in 1990 is not investment grade; the very mention of its name may reduce a wine lover to a salivating parody of a Pavlovian dog, but that's an irrelevant consideration for the cool-headed investor.

So, in order to figure out if a particular wine is IGW we have to look at its price history; IGWs show dramatic increase in price over time. All of the following questions are important; and though you may not know it, the answers are easily obtainable.

□ What price does the wine generally command at auction?

□ Does the vineyard or winery consistently produce fine wine?

□ Does the wine usually make its first retail appearance at a low in price, then increase in value over time?

□ During the forty years since the end of the Second World War, how many years has the vineyard or winery produced IGW?

- Has the wine ever sold for over $500 (or $1,000 or $10,000) per case at the time of resale?

- How many times has the vineyard or estate produced wine which annually increased in value by ten percent (or fifty or one hundred percent) over ten years?

- How does the estate or vineyard's output compare to other vineyards in the same geographical area and climate?

Consistency in price increases is almost as important as evidence of increase itself. You should also be aware that a breathtakingly expensive price does not necessarily denote a good investment. In 1961, Lafite was a good investment at $80 per case; today the same case is well over $4,800. Had you bought Lafite in the early sixties you would have made a very good investment, but if you were thinking about buying that same vintage today I would counsel you to think twice before spending your money; at $400 per bottle there's little room for the price to expand upward until at least 1990. In 1971, and again in 1983, I stopped recommending that people buy Lafite, Mouton, Pétrus, Latour, Cheval Blanc and Haut-Brion precisely because of their astronomical prices. The degree of excellence of these wines remained unchanged and high, but that wasn't the point. If a wine's purchase price is so high that it cannot reasonably increase over the coming years, it's not IGW. It's my opinion that a decent IGW should cost no more than $25 per bottle at the time of original purchase; an exceptional drinking wine, about half that price.

TYPES OF IGW. One of the easiest ways for someone not directly involved in the wine trade to unearth information about wine is through reading auction catalogues. Whether the catalogue is for Christie's, Sotheby's, Butterfield and Butterfield, the Chicago Wine Company or one of the annual charity auctions, the same wines continually reappear.

The overwhelming majority of these wines are red; most white wines simply do not age well. By far the largest number of entries are for prestigious red Bordeaux wines, followed by True Vintage Port. In the United States, you would also note the abundance of California wines offered at auction; in England, old vintage champagnes. On both sides of the Atlantic there would also be a smattering of activity in a small group of Burgundies, both red and white, one or two offerings from the Rhône, some German dessert wines (all of which are white) and a handful of Italian reds like Barbaresco and Brunello di Montalcino.

Traditionally, the investment market has focused on two types of wine: estate-bottled Bordeaux and True Vintage Port. Their longevity, their history of appreciation and the public confidence in their consistency has set these apart. Most of the Bordeaux first-growths will survive at least forty years in the better vintages; none of them will last less than fifteen years, even in the weakest vintage. The trading histories for some of these wines go back several hundred years. In 1790, Thomas Jefferson purchased some 1787 Lafite. The approximate cost per bottle, delivered to Washington, D.C., was about sixty-eight cents. In 1986, at Christie's in London, Christopher Forbes bought one of Jefferson's bottles for over $150,000. I owned a bottle of 1870 Lafite which was sensational when I opened it in 1981. Several months after this historic opening I had lunch with the Baron Elie de Rothschild, the owner of Château Lafite, and I mentioned the ancient bottle. He gave me a cool look and replied, "My dear man, you drank it too young."

Extremely long life (and high appreciation) have also made True Vintage Port a quintessential investor's favorite. Vintage Port continues improving in the bottle for fifty years or more if stored properly. In 1965, I purchased a case of 1963 Taylor for $40; as of November 1986, it was generally quoted at $1,000 per case.

Some wine lovers follow a conservative investment strategy, restricting their purchases to the great French châteaux, relying exclusively on the dozen or so blue-chip wines which fall into the category described above. But if that were the only investment avenue, or even the most practical one, you wouldn't need this book. You could choose your wines by watching *Lifestyles of the Rich and Famous.*

Unfortunately, there aren't enough of these wines to go around— at least not at prices that most of us find practical. Moreover, speculators buying in large quantities have driven the prices of many of these wines into the sky. In 1984, a Wall Street brokerage firm purchased almost 1,000 cases of the 1982 Bordeaux vintage. The firm netted a sixty-five percent profit (after taxes) one year later. This made wine the number-one collectible of the year in the firm's collectible portfolio. It also fueled an already tight market for the very top wines.

The most fertile opportunities for someone new to the investment side of wine is in the produce of less-well-known estates. The competition to obtain them is not so keen, they're more affordable, and there's greater room for price movement. You also stand the chance to make a coup; who wouldn't wish to have been one of those fortunate few who recognized the potential of Pétrus before it became the wine world's equivalent of platinum? In 1964 a client of mine purchased several cases of 1961 Château Pétrus. The price was $120 per case; in December 1985 he let one case go—for $10,000. There are other wines out there with the same potential, lesser-known French wines, probably some California wines as well.

The further afield you venture in your search for IGW the more important it becomes for you to inform yourself. I've done much of the work for you already; the last part of this chapter lists those wines whose investment potential seems clearest to me. Chapter Three explains where to go for further information. What follows is a brief discussion on what makes wines long-lived, and how the recognition factor contributes to a wine's investment value.

LONGEVITY. As wine matures it becomes more valuable without the expense of any additional processing other than storage. Furthermore, any one vintage becomes scarcer as it is drunk off, *usually prematurely*. Obviously, the longer a wine lasts the more valuable it's likely to become. The great vintages produce extremely long-lived wines; wines from 1928 are still drinking well.

I have a wealthy client in his early twenties who knows a great deal about fine wine. He once disputed my claim that a few bottles of 1870 Lafite I was selling would still taste delicious; he was convinced I was selling high-priced bottles of French vinegar. He used to needle me whenever we met: "Sold any of that vinegar lately?" To settle the argument once and for all I invited him for lunch at my apartment, where we would open a bottle—on one condition; if he liked the wine he had to purchase my remaining stock (four bottles).

I invited him inside. The bottle had been recorked at the château, but I was still nervous as I inserted the corkscrew, then eased out the long Bordeaux cork. My client smiled at me. I gently tilted the bottle and poured each of us a glass. The wine had a deep brick-amber color and a heartbreaking scent of faded violets, like the contours of youthful beauty in the face of an elegant but elderly woman.

His eyes nearly popped out his head when he tasted it. "My God, Bill, we're drinking history!"

And so we were—tasting our way back into the previous century. By way of apology he purchased my remaining four bottles. I was a little sad to see them go.

Aside from proper storage, the potential longevity of wine arises from the decisions of the winemaker during vinification. Hugh Johnson describes freshly made wine as a "complex of unresolved principles: of acids and sugars, minerals and pigments, esters and aldehydes and tannins." He goes on to explain that the finer the wine, the more it contains of all of these constituents, and the longer it takes for them to chemically harmonize. Fruity, simple wines, intended for immediate consumption, contain relatively small amounts of these brash, competitive elements.

Year-old Beaujolais makes good picnic wine because it provides a mouthful of uncomplicated fruity flavor, the taste equivalent of a bright yellow balloon. A Margaux, or meaty Cabernet from Robert Mondavi, if tasted at the same age, is a clanging pandemonium of strident impressions, each vying for attention. Predicting how a wine will resolve itself, on the basis of that early chaos, is a skill somewhere between mechanical engineering and dowsing for water. That mature wines do not always conform to the predictions made for them (good or bad) should come as no surprise.

A dozen different choices by the winemaker determine the intensity of these rival constituents. First comes the variety of grape, the quality of the vintage and the type of fermentation used in making the wine. Some grapes are higher than others in tannin, a vital ingredient for long-lived wines; Cabernet Sauvignon contains more than Merlot, for example. A château may blend its wine from Merlot and Cabernet Sauvignon in traditional proportions, but an exceptional vintage in one or the other of these grapes may cause the winemaker to rethink his traditional strategy. That ratio will affect the life of the wine. How much "press wine" should he blend with the "free-run wine"? After fermentation, about eighty percent of the wine runs out of the fermenting vat without requiring any pressing of the grapes at all; this free-run wine tends to be light and fruity. Press wine, as its name suggests, follows afterward, when the fermented grapes are pressed. Highly tannic and dark colored, press wine is added in varying percentages to wines intended for aging.

Whether or not the winemaker uses oak barrels and vats for any of these steps also affects the ultimate longevity of the wine, since tannin and vanillin leaches out of the wood into the wine, giving the vintage even greater staying power. As if all of this weren't sufficiently complicated, the origin, age and size of the oak barrel affects the amount of tannin that will seep into the wine. New oak gives off more tannin than barrels which have been used for a year or more; French oak imparts a slightly different flavor to the wine than American oak. The winemaker controls all of these variables; his skill at manipulating them establishes a dynamic whose ultimate resolution may be known only decades later.

In recent years a number of respected winemakers have begun using stainless steel tanks, part of the trend called nouveau vinification. The term refers to winemakers' responses to the needs of the market that has emerged since the wine boom in the sixties. According to Alexis Lichine, starting in the mid-sixties many winemakers began to deliberately decrease the tannin content in their wines. They accomplished this in two ways: first, by cutting back on the time they allowed the fermenting grape juice to remain in contact with the skins; and second, by reducing their use of new oak barrels (hence the arrival of stainless steel). Wines with less tannin mature faster than their heavier counterparts (and expire quicker, according to critics of nouveau vinification).

At any rate, the lighter-tannin approach has enabled vineyards to shrink the time between a vintage and its arrival in a market thirsty for drinkable wines. Purists deplore the use of stainless steel tanks, likening metal casks to tin pianos and aluminum violins, despite the fact that wines aged in metal barrels have surprised even experienced tasters.

However, until another century has passed, and we can taste a one-hundred-year-old wine aged in stainless steel (and see what such a wine fetches at auction), the question of aging in metal barrels must remain unresolved.

IGW AND AGING. Less than one percent of all wines produced in the world today can be kept for ten years or more, a minimum requirement for IGW. Once we consider a wine's price history and its reputation, the slice of wines with investment potential becomes even smaller. Relative to the world's total wine output, IGW is rare indeed. Since longevity is of critical importance in IGW, it's worthwhile to take a look at the aging process, at what happens to the wine after it's bottled.

Until as recently as the last century the chemistry of how wine ages was understood almost not at all. Our taste for aged wine has itself only developed in the last several hundred years. Before the 1700s most wines were vinified to be drunk fairly soon. The odd barrel of wine that now and then escaped everyone's notice and was allowed to sit undisturbed for several years spoiled more often than it aged. Older wines which managed to avoid bacterial contamination were treated as medicines or curative tonics, more valued for their miraculous powers of preservation (as witnessed by their proven ability to resist turning into vinegar) than for their complex of tastes. Hugh Johnson feels that the aging of wine didn't come into its own until the technology of the cork and the corkscrew came along in the fifteenth century. Even so, the popular taste still preferred coarse concoctions of young wines, raw wine fortified with brandy.

By the eighteenth century Bordeaux merchants had discovered that time improved certain of their wines. Time and motion. Bordeaux négociants often mellowed their wine by sending it on a round trip to the French colonies in the Caribbean. Nine or ten months of gentle rocking in the hold of a merchant vessel softened wines which had been unpalatably tannic the year before.

The first real scientific inquiry on the aging of wine began with Louis Pasteur. In 1863, Napoleon III and several prominent winemakers, distressed at the deterioration of their wines during travel to faraway markets, invited Pasteur to research the question of how winemakers might control the effects of aging. Pasteur himself had been born in a winemaking region, the Jura of eastern France, and he eagerly took up the challenge. After a series of experiments that involved sealing wine in glass tubes with precisely measured amounts of air he discovered that oxygen is integral to the aging process. Too much oxygen causes wine to age rapidly and turn brown; too little, and the wine doesn't age at all. Wine in half-filled test tubes aged faster than wine in full tubes, proving that too much air, too soon, will age wine to vinegar.

Oaken casks have the advantage over cement or stainless steel vats in that wood is porous; it permits the passage of air into the wine. On the negative side, wood also allows wine to evaporate. If the level of the wine in the casks isn't topped off, too much air collects in the top of the barrel, bacteria begin to grow and the wine turns to vinegar. Evaporation is part of the reason wine aged in barrels is more expensive than wine aged in stainless steel tanks. As much as twenty percent of the wine (in France, known as the angels' share) may be lost to evaporation before the wine is actually bottled.

Pasteur developed a process of heating and then cooling wine in rapid succession in order to kill microorganisms present in the wine, a technique similar to the pasteurization of milk. As an antidote to spoilage, the process is very effective. For fine wines, however, a reliance on sterile bottling practices and an emphasis on keeping the *cuverie* (fermenting room) sanitary at all times is preferable to pasteurization. *Some* bacteria are actually necessary for aging; without them, the chemical interaction of the wine's various elements takes place fitfully or not at all. Killing *all* the bacteria destroys a wine's ability to age properly, and thus become valuable.

Past discoveries that a vineyard was pasteurizing its wines have caused scandals in the wine trade. In 1930, a group of English aristocrats who had purchased 1929 Lafite sued the château when it became known that a portion of the vintage had been pasteurized. We can only imagine the horror with which the old-wine-collecting community regarded this practice. In the end, Lafite had to recall the wine and pay damages to the English. Incidentally, the fears of the English wine buyers were unfounded; I've been fortunate enough to sample the 1929 Lafite and though faded, it is still good.

A wealthy and well-known client of mine came in one day and upon entering the store purchased a bottle of the pasteurized 1929 Lafite. We talked for a few moments and he began telling me about his father's wine cellar. The old man had started collecting wines in the early 1900s, passing on the unconsumed fruits of his labor, some of which were quite rare, to his offspring.

The client told me about one of his father's most precious acquisitions—a magnum of 1858 Lafite which had once belonged to Louis Pasteur! Pasteur had received the bottle from Lafite in recognition of his service to the wine industry. My client, who had not heard of the 1930 lawsuit, was flabbergasted that quite by coincidence he had purchased one of Lafite's pasteurized wines. His own magnum, I informed him, was worth at least $25,000, and if the bottle's history and storage could be verified, perhaps as much as $100,000; a wealthy wine lover with an interest in Pasteur might have paid even more.

Pasteurized fine wine is something to beware of, if only because so many people in the fine and rare wine trade oppose the process. Thermolization and stabilization are variations on the same technique. Less expert vintners produce corpses disguised as bottled Burgundy or Bordeaux, Dorian Gray wines whose appearance after years of aging is deceptively youthful, but whose taste and bouquet are dead. Stay away from them.

THE RECOGNITION FACTOR. How does a wine establish its niche in the public consciousness? Historically famous châteaux steam along year after year with a momentum so well established that nothing short of natural disaster could unseat them from their positions in the vinous heavens. Lafite, Latour, Mouton—the legendary names evoke hours of anecdotes, of ancient wines drunk on important occasions, of fabulously expensive bottles, of celebrity patrons quaffing entire cases of the stuff at parties.

Part of the pleasure in drinking these wines is the sensation of participating in a legend. Wasn't Winston Churchill supposed to have drunk a bottle of this or that every night? Well, let's pull the cork out and see how our own impressions stack up against Winnie's. Poor old Churchill. I've heard tales linking him to champagne, red Bourdeaux, Cognac and Port, a bottle of which (depending on the particular raconteur telling the story) he was supposed to have consumed every night. Between the daily box of cigars and the gargantuan quantity of alcohol he was consuming for the future benefit of wine and spirits producers it's a wonder he managed to squeeze in any time for the war at all.

Winemakers revel in legend, as they should—mystique sells wine. Owners of vineyards go to enormous lengths to develop this cachet. Not for nothing have they developed reputations as the greatest hosts in the world. I remember tasting the 1982 Mondavi Cabernet in circumstances that were less than ideal for rational assessment. Robert Mondavi had invited a group of us for an evening's entertainment at the vineyard. We sat at picnic tables arranged among the plots of vines, sipping vintage Cabernet while Bobby Short sang from a temporary stage erected on the lawn. A dreamy California night, supper music from a premier entertainer, a bowl of stars overhead, even if a cold-blooded tasting the next day had revealed the wine to be less than appealing (it wasn't), how would I ever forget my first experience of that wine? Mondavi, in addition to his contribution to innovative production methods, is a marketing and PR genius. I'm sure thousands of other wine drinkers have been introduced to Mondavi wines under similar circumstances—and you can be damn sure that every time they introduce a friend to one of his wines, the story of their night at the vineyard gets trotted out.

Normally, I'd warn you against buying wines for investment simply because you fell in love with the vineyard, but sometimes, as in the case with Mondavi, a visit will show you if a proprietor is prepared to go the promotional distance necessary to bring his wines before the

public. In a case of a fine, but not necessarily famous wine, its investment value will often depend on whether the owner is willing to culti-
vate publicity and distribution. Tom Jordan makes great Cabernets; other
California winemakers make equally good wines, but few of them will
ever measure up to the cachet of Jordan's.

The French have long recognized that the patronage of influential
people increases the sale of their wine. When a client who has not
typically made large purchases of wine suddenly calls me with a $20,000
or $30,000 order I often discover that a visit to France recently figured
in his or her life.

Wine writers are aware of growers' penchants for entertaining even
as the writers compose "objective" accounts of tastings of new wines.
Among members of the wine trade the spring tasting tour of Bordeaux
châteaux is known as the "gout route"—an occupational hazard for
traveling wine writers and critics.

Writers themselves often provide the first wave of enthusiasm or
disappointment regarding a vintage's prospects, and with interest in wine
spreading they seem to wield more and more power. *The Wine Advocate,* by Robert Parker, Jr., mounted such a persuasive campaign in
favor of the 1982 Bordeaux vintage that members of the trade and the
public were ranting about the "vintage of the century" before the wine
was old enough to provide even a remote confirmation of his opinion.
For speculators the actual worth of the wine was almost of no consequence next to the *public perception* of its value. Not that a gulf (if there
is one) between the reputation of the 1982s and their actual worth in
terms of longevity can last for long. If the 1982s don't prove as long-
lived as some writers would have us believe, then the market will ultimately correct their price. What's important to note is the power of a
collective belief in the value of a wine.

In summary, for a wine to become IGW it must already have a
place in the public's mind, or it must have powerful backing, either the
force of an aggressive promoter—usually the grower—or a healthy endorsement from the community of wine critics. Preferably both.

LISTS OF IGW

#1 IGW

I compiled the following lists of IGW based on my experience as a wine
merchant. The major categories—#1 IGW, #2 IGW, #3 IGW—represent different degrees of risk, recognition and expense. The first group
is a collection of blue-chip wines. The reputations of these names, in
some cases, is several centuries long. Regarding French wines, the market for rare bottles from vintages in the last century attests to their

repute for longevity. The California wines have in many instances earned their reputations by dint of a long, European-style dedication to the making of fine wine. These efforts have often culminated in triumphant blind tastings in which the best of California manages to equal (or on rare occasion nudge aside) French competitors. Since these wines provide the greatest likelihood of return with the least amount of risk, they may be difficult to obtain; they are certainly the most expensive of all IGW.

BORDEAUX WINES

Château Lafite	Château Latour
Château Margaux	Château Pétrus
Château Mouton-Rothschild	Château Pichon-Lalande
Château Haut-Brion	Château Léoville-Lascases
Château La Mission-Haut-Brion	Château Ausone
Château Cheval Blanc	

BURGUNDY

Romanée-Conti	Richebourg (Domaine Romanée-Conti)
La Tâche	Le Montrachet (La Guiche or Romanée-Conti)

TRUE VINTAGE PORT

Taylor	Warre
Fonseca	Dow
Croft	Sandeman
Quinta do Noval	Cockburn
Graham	

CALIFORNIA WINES

Beaulieu Vineyard, Georges de Latour, Private Reserve Cabernet
Montelena Napa Valley Cabernet
Heitz Martha's Vineyard Cabernet
Mondavi Reserve Cabernet
Opus I

SAUTERNES AND GERMAN WINES

Château d'Yquem	Bernkasteler Doktor, Dr. Thanisch
Château Climens	Wehlener Sonnenuhr, J.J. Prum
Château Rieussec	
Château Guiraud	
Château Coutet	

#2 IGW

Wines in the second group, #2 IGW, have been culled from a broad range of classification and geography. A Bordeaux wine listed here may have been classified as a second-growth—or as a fifth. Generally, the quality of these wines is extremely close to #1 IGW, though some are perhaps not as long-lived. Although many of the French wines have had considerable stature in times past, for the most part #2 IGW have achieved their present prominence since 1960. Their trading histories, while very good, do not show the unshakable escalation of #1 IGW. But this is why they represent good value. All the #2 IGW are less expensive than #1s, with the exception of Château Palmer, in itself a sort of fluke. Palmer can be as expensive as a #1 IGW.

BORDEAUX WINES

Château Palmer	Château Lynch-Bages
Château Beychevelle	Château Trotanoy
Château Cos d'Estournel	Château La Lagune
Château Cantemerle	Domaine de Chevalier
Château Ducru-Beaucaillou	Château Figeac

CALIFORNIA WINES

Jordan Vineyard	Clos du Val Cabernet
Ridge Cabernet (Montebello)	Freemark Abbey Bosché Cabernet
Chappellet Cabernet	Sterling Cabernet
Mayacamas Cabernet	

Grgich Hills Chardonnay
Far Niente Chardonnay
Château St. Jean Chardonnay, Jean Robert Young Vineyard
Château St. Jean Johannisberg Riesling (Selected Late Harvest)
Joseph Phelps Selected Late Harvest Riesling

OTHERS

Château Suduiraut (Sauternes)
Romanée-St.-Vivant (Domaine de la Romanée-Conti)
Côte Rôtie (Guigal)
Brunello di Montalcino (Biondi-Santi)
Barbaresco (Gaja)

#3 IGW

The last category of IGW is comprised of vineyards or wines whose value is presently unsuspected. In many cases these wines have reputations of a decade or less. Fashion plays a much larger role in the acceptance of these wines than in the other categories. The list includes wines off the beaten track which I believe will nevertheless become more valuable over time. Maybe the estates once possessed a reputation, but have since fallen on hard times; a recent tasting of wine made by the new owners shows dramatic improvement. Researching the vineyard, the background of its owner, the identity and reputation of the present oenologist, the vineyard's size, location and output, all are of primary importance with #3 IGW. You're trying to predict whose reputation is most likely to improve, who's likely to make long-lived wines, which vineyard will suddenly become the darling of hip restaurateurs. The reward for this research is the satisfaction of discovering a valuable asset before it becomes well known and expensive.

BORDEAUX WINES

Château La Grave-Trigant de Boisset
Château La Gaffelière
Château Canon
Château Gloria

Château Gruaud-Larose
Château Grand-Puy-Lacoste
Château Rausan-Ségla

CALIFORNIA WINES

Rutherford Ranch
Chalone Pinot Noir
Duckhorn Merlot
Chimney Rock Cabernet

Dunn Cabernet
Sequoia Grove Estate-Bottled Cabernet
Vichon Cabernet
Dominus

VINTAGE CHAMPAGNE

Dom Perignon (white or rosé)
Pol Roger Vintage Brut
Bollinger

Krug
Roederer Cristal (white or rosé)

CHAPTER THREE

INFORMATION—WHERE TO GET IT

With hundreds of wines to choose from, the selection of even a few vineyards, whether for drinking or for investing, can seem like a daunting task. It's not. You have three very powerful resources at your disposal to help you make informed choices:

- Firsthand experience
- Your wine merchant
- Wine writing

FIRSTHAND EXPERIENCE

There's nothing like depending on your own nose when it's time to smell the coffee. One of the quickest ways to develop trust in your own judgments is to take a course in wine tasting. Courses offer structure and direction; good instructors can suggest by vivid example what to expect from different grapes, from different geographic regions and from different winemaking techniques. Courses also present wine in a format that allows comparison of different wines. Most novice wine lovers are astonished to discover that when they taste a California Chardonnay next to a white Burgundy they can actually recognize the distinct flavor of the Chardonnay grape, even though the wines come from different parts of the world and may have been vinified in very different styles. In a class you can compare your own impressions with fellow students', learning from one another.

Your sense of whether a wine tastes good or bad is your first line of defense. Never buy investment-grade wine on the basis of taste alone; but the opposite side of the coin holds just as true: nor should you allow a wine merchant or newsletter to bully you into purchasing a wine you find personally distasteful or unpleasant. Educating your palate is the only way to learn to trust your taste.

Whether you take a course or not, the important thing you can do for your own education is to develop a system that allows you to remember wine. Some people are naturally more facile at this than others; taste is the most elusive of all the senses, its impressions the most fleeting. But to become an educated wine lover you must develop a vocabulary that allows you to record your experiences. My college-age son can run rings around me when it comes to describing the taste of a particular wine. Even after almost three decades in the trade I can find myself tongue-tied when attempting to articulate the taste of a new wine. Nevertheless, I forge ahead; forcing myself to describe how a wine imprints its taste indelibly in my memory.

There are two approaches to this whole business of description. The older of the two, what I call the English School, depends on a set of terms commonly used by professionals. Red wines from Margaux, according to this methodology, often develop a scent redolent of "tobacco" or "cedar" or "cigar box." Michael Broadbent's *Wine Tasting* is an extremely useful guide to this approach. A somewhat more slippery route is the looser, metaphorical style of California. One of the funniest (and most accurate) descriptions of wine I ever encountered pertained to a modest West Coast Riesling; a wine instructor compared the experience of tasting it to "a date with a woman who sews her own clothes—nice and dependable, but you know nothing very exciting is going to happen." Most of my clients use a combination of the two, waxing metaphorical when describing their favorites, then tending to become as clinical as possible when describing why they don't care for a particular wine.

Many adult education programs offer classes in wine tasting; if possible try to enroll in an established organization devoted to wine. San Francisco and New York have wine institutes which offer a broad spectrum of training; the Academie du Vin and the International Wine Center are two that come immediately to mind. I'm pleased that the Waldorf-Astoria Hotel still offers a wine program, now in the competent hands of Harriet Lembeck, heir to Harold Grossman, the original instructor.

If you drank a different wine every day for the next ten years you couldn't sample every wine that's for sale today. Professionals who claim to be familiar with all the world's wine are talking gibberish. Even a superficial acquaintance with the worldwide variety of wines, let alone the different bottlings and vintages, would be a Sisyphean task.

Once you realize this limitation and understand there are no absolute authorities in wine beyond your own confidence, then the task of educating your palate becomes an enjoyable one. Forget all the stories you've heard about legendary palates—most of the time they're just anecdotal embroidery around a grain of snobbism. Baron Philippe de Rothschild, of Mouton-Rothschild, has been known to remark that in a blind tasting he can't tell the taste of his wine from that of his nearest neighbors'. Tasting is a skill, one that can be learned. Combined with memory, it's your primary avenue for wine appreciation; properly directed, it will make you knowledgeable about the many ways vineyards produce wine, instilling you with confidence in your own perceptions.

Taken with a grain of salt, visits to vineyards can put your impressions into perspective. Many American vineyards welcome tourists. Napa Valley is second only to Disneyland in the number of its annual visitors. If you're in France, Italy or Germany, plan ahead; European vineyards often accommodate visitors, but not on the spur of the moment. A phone call or letter in advance of your visit may earn you an invitation, and a tour with someone who speaks English. On rare occasions you may even have the opportunity to speak to the winemaker, although many of them tend to flee as soon as they see a car pulling into the drive. A friend of mine on his honeymoon visited Romanée-Conti with his bride. The cellarmaster was so enchanted with the newlyweds that he kept them for eight hours, bringing out one old Burgundy after another. My friend and his wife were a little disoriented by the end of the tasting; they fell into their car, headed down the driveway and ran right into the gatepost.

Vineyards and wineries often provide facilities for tasting their wines. First-rate operations paint their tasting rooms white (so you can get an accurate idea of the wine's color). If no one offers you a spittoon, ask for one. You're not obliged to swallow the wine you taste, and if you're spending a day touring wineries it's more than a question of restraint—it's a matter of survival. When tasting out of doors it's perfectly acceptable to spit the wine onto the ground.

You can enlarge your firsthand experience with wine by becoming part of your local wine community. If you have a favorite restaurant, introduce yourself to the wine steward. Get to know the wine merchant where you buy wine, even if you don't feel particularly inclined to take his advice. Most large cities have societies or organizations devoted to the love of wine. Many European organizations—Les Amis du Vin, La Chaine des Rotisseurs and Chevaliers du Tastevin—have American branches with active and informed memberships, often with a lively mix of enthusiastic wine lovers and members of the trade. Becoming involved with such an organization is a helpful way to become part of the grapevine, to hear about what other people are drinking (or perhaps laying down for investment).

No matter how informally you attempt to pursue firsthand knowledge, it's best to have at least one strategy: limit yourself. It's possible, given enough time, to superficially acquaint yourself with thousands of wines. But why not get to know several hundred wines well? For the sake of your own interest and enlightenment, instead of just tasting every wine at random, restrict some of your efforts to a predetermined plan—the wines of one geographic area or grape variety. Try making yourself an expert in the wines of St.-Estèphe or in Cabernets from Napa and Sonoma.

MERCHANTS

If people put half as much thought into choosing a wine merchant as they did into finding a good restaurant, they'd be happy with the wine they bought and well informed at the same time. We've turned into such efficient consumers that we've lost sight of trust, the basis for any satisfying merchant-client relationship. I know people who read their favorite wine reviewer and then frantically telephone all over New York to find the recommended wines. People who depend on reviews to make their decisions ignore the experts who are closer at hand—their neighborhood wine merchant. If I'm sitting in a hospital waiting room and I find an article in a medical journal about my particular problem I'm going to read it, but I'm still going to talk to the doctor; there's nothing like a second opinion, in wine or in life.

Merchants have the inside track on wine information—the latest word on growers, oenologists, distribution and importation problems, as well as published wine reports. They are, from the client's perspective, one step closer to the winemaking process. The sharp wine lover will utilize them.

Consider the tale of Michel Delon, proprietor of Chateau Léoville-Las-Cases in Bordeaux. After harvesting and bottling, he releases his wines in stages in order to create scarcity and thereby drive the prices up. In fact he only offered about half of the 1983 vintage for sale in 1984; he intends to release the remainder slowly, over the next twenty years. If importers receive lower quantities of wine than they request, then they have less to sell and will therefore have to charge more. This, Delon claims, keeps his image up. (When Bordeaux proprietors start talking about their wine's image, they usually mean it's time to push the price up.) Léoville-Lascases is not alone in this practice. Many of the other famous châteaux do the same thing; they drive the price up by spurious means, to whatever heights the market will bear.

This is the sort of situation that makes a wine merchant invaluable. It's possible to look up the number of cases that Léoville-Lascases produces each year, but it takes a member of the trade to figure out how much wine the château made *this* year and how many have thus far been released. Is the wine actually scarce or is there an artificial shortage? This is where it gets tricky for the investor attempting to operate alone and unadvised. Finding out this kind of information is a good wine merchant's job. I remember a client who recently wanted to trade some of his cases of 1976 Jordan Cabernet for a more recent vintage. He was willing to offer me a five-to-one swap; five of the 1982 Cabernet for one case of his 1976. I telephoned Tom Jordan and asked him about his 1976 Cabernet (which had been a lovely wine). He was quite candid about the fact that he'd made his first wines in an easy, accessible style so that people would drink them, thereby helping to promote his reputation; but the wines didn't have the tannins to make them last. The 1976, he concluded, would not be long for this world.

Rather generously (I thought), I offered to swap one case of 1982 for a single case of the client's 1976. He barked something obscene into his end of the telephone and hung up; he's probably still sitting on his cases of 1976 Jordan, waiting to pounce on some unwary investor who'll think he's getting a great deal on a famous California wine.

In addition to information, a good relationship with a merchant will get you access to IGW that comes his way in small quantities. I keep a list of special customers who I know will always be interested in whatever rare wines I come across. Before those wines are even advertised, these customers know about them. Most merchants keep such lists handy for special opportunities, and a fair amount of IGW disappears into the cellars of preferred clients without the public even becoming aware it existed.

All wine merchants are not created equal. An inexperienced one can cost you money, especially if you're buying futures (discussed later), so take care to keep your eye out for the following signs:

□ Is the place clean? Does someone care enough to make sure the aisles are swept and the bottles dusted? Filthy bottles are only appealing in old black and white movies, not in a wine store. Are the bottles on display in a reclining position? Is there mention of rotation of bin bottles that are standing for display purposes? Do you get the feeling that you are in an establishment with the right feel for wine? A merchant who devotes a lot of space to liquor displays may not be the best choice for a futures sale.

□ Is there a diverse selection? If a store's entire stock is upper-crust red Bordeaux, or low-end California, then most likely the merchant is either unable or perhaps unwilling to do the legwork necessary to find original wines. Likewise beware of discount wine stores. Most of these shops are purchasing closeouts and deal with three or four middlemen. These wines are okay, but they lack the magic that's supposed to be part of the relationship with your merchant—you're not buying wine because you're thirsty. Some discounters are willing to develop personal relationships with their customers, but in the end, you get what you pay for. Price reductions are fine, but it's not only the price that's being reduced.

□ Is there inexpensive wine? Inexpensive wine may be a good or a bad sign. An offering of unusual Rioja wines indicates a merchant is willing to take some trouble to seek out unusual bargains for his clientele; a store with a half dozen floor displays of $3 jug wine does not. The staff of a decent shop should be as keen for their recent $5 discovery as they are for their single bottle of 1959 Lafite.

▫ Is the staff informed and enthusiastic? A good wine shop radiates an aura of interest, of energy. Ask questions about the bottles on the shelf. Are people informed or just interested in selling you something? Probably only five percent of places that sell wine are in fact knowledgeable purveyors of wine. Ask questions, judge for yourself.

▫ What kind of lighting does the store have? Is it grocery store illumination? Direct fluorescent lighting permanently discolors wine and causes the taste to go "off." Eventually the wine browns or "madeirizes." Is this any way to treat a wine in a display area? If wine is treated poorly in the display area how can you expect it to be treated any differently in the merchant's storage facility? Sometimes you may be better off paying a slightly higher price simply for the assurance that the wine you're buying has been treated correctly. It's amazing how a case of wine purchased for $200 from a serious wine merchant can taste infinitely superior to the same case purchased for $180 at the corner liquor store or nearby supermarket.

▫ Does the store send out a newsletter? Does the newsletter inform you? A catalogue or newsletter tells you a lot about the personality of the shop. I know of several discount operations that behave as if they were selling computer hardware. They generally list up to a thousand wines without commentary—except to say that their prices are the lowest.

▫ Is the merchant open to questions? Credentials, time and experience are at work in a wine shop. Don't be afraid to ask how long a store has been in business. If they're selling futures, ask how many years of experience they've had.

▫ Is the merchant a good judge of character? Remember, when a merchant contracts to buy a wine, he's buying an extension of the winemaker's soul. If your merchant doesn't seem to care much for people, beware.

▫ Is the merchant also an importer? Most likely he won't be, but if he is, it's a good sign: first, that his prices don't reflect markups from excessive middlemen; and second, that he deals directly with *négociants* or proprietors, so he'll have information about the wine directly from the horse's mouth. Look for wines with the merchant's name and address on them. Sometimes this information will be affixed on a strip label directly below the regular label. If a merchant claims he is an importer, ask him how often he brings in new wines.

▫ How good are the merchant's recommendations? If everything else checks out, go ahead and try ten or fifteen of his suggested wines. Never ask for advice about investment wine from a merchant who can't provide you with wine you like to drink. Let's face it, if you're a serious wine lover you're likely to spend quite a bit of money on wine, even if you never consider investment. A fundamental compatibility ought to exist between you and a merchant; if it's not there, go someplace else.

WINE WRITING

The bibliography at the rear of this volume lists the books I've found particularly valuable. I strongly suggest that you acquire at least two basic references: Alexis Lichine's *New Encyclopedia of Wines and Spirits* (1984) and Hugh Johnson's *World Atlas of Wine* (1985). These books will give you all the structure you need for an elaborate education in wine. Lichine's *Encyclopedia* is the classic general-audience reference, with articles on all aspects of winemaking, including the lore and history of individual vineyards. Where else will you get the definitive treatment on the chief wine-growing districts in Yugoslavia? For a map of the Yugoslavian wine districts, open up Hugh Johnson's *Atlas*. Both of these volumes are seductive to professional and novice alike. Though you may start out intending to look up one quick detail (e.g. how to spell "Meursault"), you can become easily entangled in the legends of winemaking or tying to fingerwalk your way through the Côte de Nuits.

The most current information about wines and vineyards appears in a blizzard of magazines and newsletters. Ten years ago there were two contenders in the field, *The French Wine Review* and *Decanter*, and the world was a much simpler place. When wine periodicals began to proliferate toward the end of the last decade I felt an obligation to keep abreast of as many of them as possible and I suddenly found myself getting three new wine reviews every day. Quite without warning I was becoming an information junkie, poring over the latest heap of disposable data, desperately sifting for the truth in a quagmire of ridiculously obscure terminology.

No more. Now I'm like a man who, once addicted to swimming, enjoys sitting on the end of the dock and dangling his feet in the water. I see all of the reviews in turn, but I may only catch any individual periodical every five or six months. I have problems with reviews, with the self-importance of so many wine writers, with the descriptive jargon that gives me lockjaw. If I were writing a newsletter I'd call it *Down to Earth* by Blue-Sky Bill. In my opinion the arcane jargon of newsletters and the obsessive rating systems encourage all of the worst things about wine—snobbery, exclusivity, intimidation and fear. Newsletters turn wine lovers into monsters. Lord knows I've endured many a dinner, clamping my mouth shut while some twit next to me attempted to palm off the latest review as his own informed opinion.

Is there any hope?

Yes, if you're confident. Don't allow newsletters to bamboozle you; you have two other sources of information at hand, your own experience and that of your wine merchant. Treat newsletters like inexpensive house plants; if they don't work or you don't like them, throw them away. Your purpose in buying a newsletter is to enlighten yourself, to clarify your understanding. If a newsletter doesn't serve that purpose, it's probably the periodical's fault, not yours.

Read one copy of a periodical. If you're happy, then try to find how many of the reviewed wines are available. If you can't get the wine, why read the publication again? Newsletters and magazines should describe available wine in easily understood terms.

Here's a quick overview of some of the more popular wine periodicals.

The New York Wine Companion. 210 Fifth Avenue, Suite 1102, New York, NY 10011; (212) 683-9221. This is a recent arrival, but it looks reasonably sane. Monthly interviews with a person from the trade; reviews wines in shops and wine bars around New York. Keeps reviews down to thirty wines a month, most generally under $10.

The Underground Newsletter. P.O. Box 3700, Seal Beach, CA 90740; (213) 430-2284. John Tilson reviews upper-level, expensive wines. Tends to use esoteric terminology. Finding some of these wines can be a problem. I think it's probably less the newsletter's fault than distribution problems with very expensive wines. Good publication for a limited market.

The New York Wine Cellar. P.O. Box 392, Prince Station, New York, NY 10012; (212) 260-5306. This is an indispensable tool for someone who buys a lot of wine in New York, or just wants to keep abreast of retail prices. The NYWC provides some general market advice (when to buy futures, when to hold off, etc.), along with an interview with someone from the trade, a critic, proprietor or whoever. The guts of the letter is its great consumer guide for locating wines. It gives the lowest available price for specific wines and tells where to find them. Also lists places where the wine may be purchased within fifteen percent of the lowest price. Call ahead to make sure of availability.

The Wine Advocate. 1002 Hillside View, Parkton, MD 21120; (301) 329-6477. Here it is, the *hot* newsletter for investors with money to burn. Robert Parker is unassailably the leading wine critic for aficionados of upper-crust wine. This man can claim to have fired the first shot in the explosion of praise for the 1982s. He has a tendency to review expensive wines with limited availability.

The Wine Review. 3119 Jackson Street, San Francisco, CA 94115; (415) 922-2755. Claude Kolm writes a letter similar in style to Robert Parker's, but he's a strong believer in price-value relationship. His reviews are influenced by price as well as taste. He also provides an interesting monthly economic analysis of the wine market. This man has a devoted following in California that can only grow as more wine lovers discover him.

The Wine Investor. 6515 Sunset Boulevard, Suite 300B, Los Angeles, CA 90028, (213) 461-9437. Although the *WI* is completely trade-oriented, Paul Gillette provides an interesting, lighthearted (but sophisticated) look at the overall wine market. He doesn't review individual wines, rather discusses overall market trends, such as the effect of coolers on the market. It's actually a well-written market letter.

The Vine. P.O. Box 48414, Chicago, IL 60648; telephone in England—01-579-3877. Clive Coates is a former writer for *Decanter.* Each issue contains a wonderful in-depth review of a single property. He supplies extensive historical perspective on vineyards, their wines, owners, reputations, price, and other subjects. His investment analysis is trenchant and not to be dismissed lightly. His prose is graceful and his explanations accessible even to novice wine buffs.

International Wine Review. P.O. Box 285, Ithaca, NY 14851; (607) 273-6071. *IWR* arranges extensive roundtable tastings with clinical comments by members of the trade. Straightforward articles on wine-related topics by Craig Goldwyn. Outstanding.

Decanter. Saint John's Chambers, 2-10 Saint John's Road, London SW11 1PN England. English, humorous, features on different wines every month, lively letters-to-the-editor section. Michael Broadbent presents a monthly column of "Tasting Notes." One of the chief advantages of *Decanter* is an extremely useful monthly price index. The index shows the previous month's auction prices, as well as gives the two most recent auction prices (in pounds). A grand, terrific magazine; serious, without being self-important.

Finigan Wine Letter. 1700 Broadway, New York, NY 10019, (212) 956-6381. Robert Finigan is back in harness after a two-year hiatus. Finigan was almost unique in advising his readers *not* to purchase the 1982 Bordeaux vintage. Good taste and common sense reviews.

W.I.N.O. Newsletter/The Wine Trader. 881 Sneath Lane, #114, San Bruno, CA 94066; (415) 588-9463. Editor, Linda E. Mead. W.I.N.O. (Wine Investigation for Novices and Oenophiles) is actually a wine club with two helpful publications—the *Newsletter* and the *Trader.* The former, which accepts no paid advertising, runs general interest articles pertaining to wine appreciation as well as describing the activities of various W.I.N.O. chapters. The *Trader,* on the other hand, makes no bones about its function as a vehicle for advertising. However, nestled among the reproductions of labels and exhortations to try this or that wine, you'll find some valuable information—lists of wineries and vineyards offering their own newsletters, and a section offering free advertising space to private consumers wishing to buy, swap or sell wine.

The Wine Spectator. 400 East 51st Street, New York, NY 10022; (212) 751-6500. This is the *New York Times* of the wine world. A large newsprint magazine, it offers reviews, interviews with people in the trade, serious articles on market conditions and wine philosophy. Very heavily distributed.

Auction catalogues are also a worthwhile, though imprecise, method of keeping track of prices. You can obtain information about subscribing to catalogues by writing to the auction houses listed in Chapter Eight.

CHAPTER FOUR

STRATEGY OF WINE INVESTING

ATTITUDE

There's a man who comes into my store and buys Château Latour for his dog; he claims that the dog not only distinguishes between Latour and less expensive wines, but that he also refuses to allow his master to fob off inferior vintages of his preferred château.

People buy wine for a host of reasons unconnected with their wine-drinking pleasure, including investment. Before you actually run out to your neighborhood wine merchant in hopes of becoming the first guy on your block to own a case of Château Pétrus, take a minute to examine your motives.

More than one wine lover has been bitten by the investment bug. Too much of any good thing will not only corrupt your ability to simply enjoy wine, any wine, but you will also risk losing your most valuable asset, a level head.

I have another client who buys nothing but #1 IGW. The cachet of wine investing has completely seduced him. Despite a magnificent wine cellar, his greatest joy is not in tasting and sharing his precious collection of liquid beauties, but in putting his co-workers to shame when the topic of investments arises in conversation. He shivers with anticipation when somebody says something like, "I did pretty well in commodities last year."

"That so?" my client replies. "Just *how* well did you do?"

"About twenty percent, mostly in pork and wheat futures. What about you?"

"Oh, I never play the commodities market," my client says, pausing just long enough to allow everyone to think he's probably too meek to invest in anything except a passbook savings account. "I got about a hundred percent return last year, mostly Château Latour, but I threw in some Lafite and one case of Ausone for good measure."

My client cackles with glee as he describes the collective intake of breath, the barrage of questions. Latour? Lafite? You own that stuff?

Some people consider this behavior the worst sort of name-dropping. They maintain it's just one more variation on the aesthete wine lover swooning over his glass of claret: substitute "rate of return" and "compound value" for "the exquisite sentimentality of violets in the early nose" and you've got the same animal. I won't presume to judge, except to say that this particular client has let his satisfaction cloud his sense. He's made some astute selections at a time when prices are jumping, but he's so addicted to impressive short-term gains that he's headed for a tumble. The wine market, like any other investment forum, slumps periodically, and the ones to suffer most from these hiccups are short-term investors.

Go ahead, if you like: buy wine for status, for ego-gratification, to win a lover, feed your dog or impress your friends, but don't confuse such purchases with investment. From my perspective there are two reasons for buying wine:
1) For the pleasure of drinking.
2) To finance the pleasure of drinking.
Anything else is peripheral to the subject of wine investment.

MAKING PURCHASES

Rule Number One: Stick to my lists of IGW.
It's been my experience that it takes a while for most people to get in the habit of distinguishing between IGW and drinking wines. For my purposes, anything that is *not* IGW is a drinking wine. The previous chapters emphasized formal distinctions between wines that taste good and wines that make money. Learn to think of IGW as a commodity, a commodity that you can trade and whose trading will enhance your drinking pleasure of other wines.

Ironically, the very qualities which have contributed to some Bordeaux wines' success as investment vehicles, their mystique, their popular reputations for occult complexity, inhibit many wine lovers from thinking of them as investments. Instead they continue to regard them as drinking wines, albeit drinking wines for those with deeper pockets and more sophisticated palates than themselves.

Not so. Wine knowledge certainly has its specialized aspects, but you needn't master those aspects to become a successful investor. Nor should the exalted position of certain châteaux in the pantheon of wine inhibit you from buying them as investments. If it helps, think of IGW as financial building blocks in the elevation of your own cellar.

The biggest mistake of wine lovers new to investing is their insistence on purchasing wines which will not appreciate. The criteria for IGW, as we've seen, are simple and straightforward: the wine must be long-lived, it must be of high quality and it must have an international reputation not only for prestige, but as a tradeable commodity. If you compromise these standards then you compromise your investment.

Every wine lover has his or her treasured favorites, the obscure *cru bourgeois*, the *petit château* from Bourg or Blaye, the Zinfandel discovered while driving through the Carneros district. One of President Reagan's favorite wines is a Parducci Cabernet-Merlot (I know because he called me personally to complain that I hadn't delivered it). He told me that he and Mrs. Reagan had liked the wine ever since they'd spent an afternoon touring the winery when he was still governor of California. Another client, a physician who vacations in Europe with his wife, purchased Schloss Vollrads from me. On one trip they stayed in Wiesbaden. On their first day they spent the morning soaking in the spa's mineral baths, then made the short drive to Winkel and toured the vineyard at Schloss Vollrads, returning to Wiesbaden that evening for dinner and a night at the casino.

Any wines first encountered under such circumstances have an enduring charm and appeal.

Quite naturally we'd like to nudge these favorites onto the list of IGWs, to see them elevated in the eyes of the world to their rightful stature (and see our own pioneering cleverness validated in the investment arena). But this sort of logic confuses apples and oranges. If a wine doesn't meet the criteria spelled out in Chapter Two (or isn't likely to in the near future), then it isn't IGW.

Likewise, some wine lovers delight in seeking out small estates, and finding one whose taste seems out of proportion to its price, think they've discovered a future IGW. Perhaps they have, but much more information should be considered before passing judgment. Are other people talking about the wine? Does it have a production large enough to establish a market, or is it so small that it will never likely get the circulation necessary to assist its reputation? Is the proprietor, winemaker or manager of the estate a significant figure willing to publicize and push the wine until it impresses itself upon the public palate? Is there anything about the specific vineyard which would lead you to believe its wines will soon develop into collector's items, generating a history of being traded? For the selections of the wine drinker fresh to investment the answer is almost always no.

Clients argue with me on this point, especially regarding second labels from famous houses since these wines seem like obvious candidates for future elevation. If Latour and Lafite are #1 IGW, don't Les Forts de Latour and Moulin des Carruades, the second wines of these estates, deserve at least a place on the #3 IGW list?

In a word, no. Second wines are undoubtedly great values from the standpoint of the wine-loving consumer; but they're *second* for a reason—they're not good enough to be *first*. By definition, second wine does not meet the standards of the estate's first wine. There may be several reasons for this: perhaps the wine came from a plot that didn't do as well as the rest of the estate's holdings, or as is most frequently the case, from vines that are not yet mature. Second wines often come from the youngest vines in the vineyard. Although experts disagree over how old a vine must be before it yields wine that will age well, the range is roughly eight to twelve years. Second wines are usually drunk younger than their older and more distinguished siblings and they may provide a fascinating insight into the winemaker's skill at a famous château, but they are not material for investment.

Nor should you assume that simply because a professional wine writer recommends a wine for drinking that the wine qualifies as IGW. Some wine columnists consistently recommend unobtainable wines. You might read the critic's endorsement, and go to several wineshops and merchants, only to have them tell you that the wine is only rarely available—not a good sign for a future IGW trying to make an impression on the market. A prominent New York restaurant critic once mentioned a California Chardonnay we happened to carry. Avid readers bought our entire stock in a single day; since the vineyard was a small boutique operation we had no hope of replenishing our supply. Latecomers could only console themselves with the admonition to get up earlier the next time they wanted a fashionable wine. By all means, avail yourself of critics' suggestions, especially if you find your own taste confirming a particular critic's observations. But don't assume that a critic's imprimatur will elevate wine to the ranks of IGW—or even make the wine easily available for purchase.

If you're the sort of wine lover who absolutely *must* cut his own path, even regarding investment wines, then look for small vineyards also owned by the proprietor of a large estate, or connected in some way with the same winemaker. La Grave-Trigant-de-Boisset, for example, is owned by Christian Mouiex. Christian's father, Jean-Pierre, is the part-owner of Pétrus. The Mouiex family brings a singular dedication to their work, and any vineyard associated with them is bound to flourish.

Rule Number Two: Never buy on the basis of taste alone.

Someone once asked Harry Waugh, the famous wine writer and critic, when he last mistook a Burgundy for a Bordeaux. Waugh replied, "Not since lunch."

A developed palate is a wonderful asset to successful wine investment, as long as you keep it in its place. Wine writers often confuse taste with price. Taste is not the only measure of a good value, and from the standpoint of investment it's almost secondary. Some excellent IGW tastes pitiful during its first years of existence because aging is what improves its taste and increases its value. For example, I tasted a 1979 Château Peyrabon in July 1980. It was undrinkable. Mainly it tasted of deep, impenetrable tar. By late October of the same year, the same wine was a scintillating, joyous surprise, with wave after wave of youthful, deep fruit rolling across my tongue.

Investment considerations aside, I'm frequently asked why someone should buy expensive wine. Does expensive wine taste better than inexpensive wine? In the short run, generally not. IGW is made to last a long, long time. The high tannin content of young IGWs often (although not always) makes them taste leathery and astringent, leaving your mouth feeling as though you'd just gargled with overbrewed tea. Particularly powerful vintages can take a decade to mellow, before allowing the more appealing features of their taste to assert themselves.

Some exceptional vintages, or specific wines within a vintage, do manage to combine immediate drinkability with an ability to age. Wine critics who favored the 1982s (I'm still not convinced) singled them out for that specific reason. By comparison to the pleasurable 1982s, wines from the vintage of the following year, the 1983s, taste like tough customers indeed. Two superior vintages appearing back-to-back, each highly unlike the other: wine writers have dubbed the 1982s "precocious," meaning they're pleasant to drink years ahead of the time one would expect; the 1983s, on the other hand, are "classically structured," an allusion to the sort of wine that everyone thinks Bordeaux used to make in the good old days before nouveau vinification.

Predicting how young wine will taste in future years is a notoriously tricky business, the confidence of some wine writers notwithstanding. The great wines of 1961, another "classically structured" vintage, were followed by the easy-drinking 1962s, wines whose early palatability caused many writers to predict they wouldn't last. Nevertheless, I sometimes find myself tasting a 1962 that's still wonderful, still capable of proving the critics wrong. Perhaps the 1982s will upset my predictions as well.

Rule Number Three: Buy good wine in good years.

The wisdom of this would seem obvious, but speculative frenzy—the fear of being shut out of a boom market—tempts many novice wine buyers to consider buying wines even from off vintages (assuming the year hasn't been a total disaster). Technology has so weighted the odds in the winemakers' favor that only extreme bad weather can ensure a truly catastrophic vintage. Taking this as their cue, buyers mistakenly continue to pay the high prices demanded by vineyards for inferior vintages, assuming that high opening prices guarantee the wine will appreciate in value, just as its more highly regarded predecessors.

Exceptional wines may be found in almost any vintage, wines whose taste runs completely counter to the trend that year. Don't mistake them for IGW, however; the buyer of the future is much more likely to assume that your wines from each vintage, good and bad, will adhere to the vintage style rather than run counter to it. In the case of an exception, the burden of proof will be on you, as the seller, to demonstrate the wine's superiority.

Speculation in inferior vintages contributed to the market break of the early seventies. Buyers snapped up 1971s, 1972s (which received incredible hype and then turned out to be duds) and 1973s without regard for the quality of these wines. Investors forgot that wine's value doesn't exist in a vacuum; presumably at the end of a long chain of investors is someone who's willing to pay a fabulous price to drink the wine. It began to dawn on investors in 1974 that maybe the drinkers of these wines existed more vividly in their imaginations than in fact, an insight borne out by one buyer after another dumping his stocks over the following months.

Off years sometimes provide bargains, especially in the ranks below the first- and second-growths. Buy them for drinking, not investing.

Rule Number Four: Physically inspect your wine.
Demand clarity in your claret. Hold the wine up to a bright light and don't purchase it if you see cloudiness or a lot of sediment. Some light sediment is normal; excessive sediment signals a poorly made wine. Likewise beware of leaking corks or gummy residue around the bottom of the lead capsule covering the cork, an indication of poor corking or improper maintenance of the wine.

Opportunities to inspect wine before purchasing it vary according to the circumstances of sale. A reputable wine merchant will always allow you to inspect wine before taking delivery. Wine sold at auction is frequently *not* available for physical inspection and you have to rely on the description in the catalogues. Michael Davis, in charge of Christie's wine auctions in the United States, assured me that he tries to be "brutally honest," in describing the color of the wine and the condition of the bottle. Nevertheless, you should never pass up the chance to inspect wine before buying it.

Infrequently, auctions will offer wine for inspection, and even tasting, by investors who express a serious interest in buying. The opportunity to taste a thimbleful of rare wine was a big attraction at the Heublein Rare Wine Auctions, until Heublein discontinued them several years ago. The small size of lots offered at auction (sometimes just a few bottles) and the logistics of making such samples available to large groups of bidders almost always precludes the luxury of tasting.

Never buy wine from a private collector without physically inspecting it unless you're personally familiar with his or her cellar. In an ideal world, we wouldn't need such inspection, but the possibility of destructive storage conditions makes it a necessity. Also, since such transactions are against the law in most states (an obstacle which hasn't impinged on trading thus far), in the event the wine turns out to be bad your legal recourse is limited.

Along similar lines, make sure that you know the policy of your wine merchant regarding unfit wine. Many auction houses spell out their policy regarding unsatisfactory wine in the front of their catalogues. If you don't see such an explanation, ask for it.

Rule Number Five: Know the wine's provenance before you buy.

"Provenance" is the history of the wine's ownership. Knowing who owned the wine before you bought it is an invaluable indication of the care the wine has received until now. A wine that originated in an English cellar, then found its way to New York, then journeyed across country to the home of a San Francisco collector has done a great deal of traveling. Vibration, movement and excessive temperature changes seriously diminish the longevity of IGW. Unknown provenance can be more of a problem at auctions than with a trusted wine merchant. An accurate travel history is more often available from a merchant than an auctioneer, mainly because the merchant is dealing in more recent vintages and he tends to be the first line of retail supply. The longer a wine has been around and the more times it has changed hands, the greater the likelihood it has encountered some negative influence, and the smaller the probability that such information will be made known to you. When you purchase a bottle or case, there is sometimes no way of knowing whether it came directly from the château, or whether it was shipped from France to California to Chicago to London and then to New York. Be prepared to pay more for wine that's been moved only once. It's an additional assurance that your investment is still worthwhile.

Rule Number Six: Never buy wine from someone you don't trust.

Fraud and forgery are nothing new to the wine trade. A plague of ersatz clarets, phony chablis and fake champagne motivated the French government to form the Institut National des Appellations d'Origine, an organization dedicated to the strict definition of both wine regions and the types of winemaking techniques available to the growers within that region. California still manages to pump out its jugs of "burgundy" and "chablis," but nobody with any wine knowledge at all would confuse these screwtop variants with their French namesakes.

Where fine wine is concerned, the situation is not so clear. The sale of fine wine is a golden opportunity for a swindler. What other product is sold with the understanding that it won't be "functional" for ten years? Regard bargain offers of fine wine with extreme skepticism—advice that was pertinent to the New York market in 1982.

A fraud perpetrated that year concerned the sale of imitation 1975 Château Mouton-Rothschild. Among agents of the Bureau of Alcohol,

Tobacco and Firearms, and members of the wine trade, the incident is known as the Great Wine Sting. The scam began in California, where Louis Feliciano, working in his Sausalito apartment, filled several thousand Bordeaux-style bottles with cheap red wine he had purchased in bulk. An unwitting printer supplied him with custom-made "wallpaper" featuring sharply detailed reproductions of the Mouton-Rothschild label. Feliciano scissored the labels out of the pattern and glued them to the bottles. Voilà! Château Mouton-Rothschild, at a fraction of the real wine's cost.

The con artist shipped about forty cases of the bogus Mouton to a house he owned in Parlin, New Jersey. Operating with a local accomplice, a computer salesman called John Robinson, he began approaching New York wine merchants with a deal he thought they couldn't refuse: 1975 Mouton for $250–$300 per case, an absurdly low price for the hard-to-get vintage.

Even in the bull market of 1982 retailers must have smelled something suspicious about the offer, because by the time Feliciano and Robinson approached me the offer was for 10,000 bottles at $8 apiece, less than a fifth of the going rate for genuine 1975 Mouton. The pair also ran ads in the *New York Times* offering "imitation" Mouton for sale, although I didn't know that at the time. I accepted a sample bottle of the bargain first-growth and sent it to the Buckingham Corporation, the U.S. importer of Mouton. Buckingham immediately identified the wine as a fraud. With BATF agents posing as interested investors, I set up a second meeting with Feliciano. The agents purchased eleven cases of the fake Mouton from Feliciano; they also bought a batch from Robinson at a second sale. Both men were arrested; all of the fraudulent wine was recovered and destroyed; Feliciano and Robinson were charged with selling alcoholic beverages without a wholesaler's tax stamp.

Feliciano's price was what tipped me off—not the appearance of the bottles. The reproduction of the labels was unnervingly accurate (when Feliciano was arrested he still owed the printer $3,000 for his "wallpaper"). As awareness of wine's investment value spreads, I'm sure the temptation will become greater and greater for unscrupulous individuals to attempt this sort of scheme, requiring wine lovers to be extra vigilant.

Present laws forbidding resale of fine wine between collectors further encourages fraud. Collectors quite naturally feel that they ought to have the right to do with their wine as they please, including selling it back to a retailer or to another collector. These types of transactions take place all the time. Wine lovers engaging in such transactions should insist upon an appraisal from a bona fide wine expert before committing to such a purchase. If what's in the bottle turns out not be what's on the label, you have no legal recourse. By the way, I still have one bottle of the fake Mouton. Once in a while, in order to demonstrate the seriousness of the problem, I invite a dinner guest to attempt to distinguish between the counterfeit and the real thing. Everybody guesses correctly about fifty percent of the time, not a very good average for investment purchases.

Rule Number Seven: Buy cases and large bottles.
This is a good rule of thumb, anecdotes about individual bottles of *rare* wine notwithstanding. The market for single bottles of fine wine is small (and the operant word here is *fine*, not *rare*); the evidence can be gleaned from the pages of any wine auction catalogue. A dozen standard-sized bottles of fine wine (750 ml each), sold individually, do not collectively equal the selling price of a single intact case of the same wine in the same vintage—and there's the added difficulty of selling one bottle at a time. Wine in its original case often receives a premium of an additional twenty percent, just as a rare stamp still attached to an envelope canceled "First Day of Issue" has more value than one torn from the corner of an anonymous envelope.

In general, buy cases, and try to buy at least two cases of everything—one for keeping in the original case, where it is more valuable than if moved anywhere else, and one for potential drinking and trading.

The exception to the case-only rule is with magnums and other oversize bottles. Not only does wine age more slowly in large bottles, but the bottles themselves exert an unusual attraction. A cellar of magnums, double magnums and imperials has a weird sort of magical appeal, like stumbling into a cave of sleeping giants, an appeal corroborated in the market. In 1968 a friend of mine purchased a double magnum of 1961 Pétrus for $400, a fortune in the late sixties. People thought he had parted ways with his senses until he sold it in 1972 for $13,000. I expect the large-bottle market to boom in the 1990s, although my friend hopes that no one else finds out about it.

Bottle sizes run as follows:

> Standard bottle—750 milliliters (¾ of a liter)
> Liter bottle—1,000 ml
> Magnum—1.5 liters or 2 × standard bottle
> Double Magnum—3 liters or 4 × standard bottle
> Jeroboam—5 liters or approximately 6⅔ × standard bottle
> Imperial—6 liters or 8 × standard bottle bottle

Vineyards produce oversize bottles in very limited quantities. The larger the bottle, the smaller its production. Bottles larger than magnums are often inconvenient to store because the size of the wine's case doesn't match the standard-bottle case, but the return on large bottles, if you can find them, makes it all worthwhile. One of my clients requested Tom Jordan of Jordan Vineyards to specially bottle six imperials of Jordan Cabernet for him, an investment that I'm sure will repay him royally.

Don't buy half-bottles; they age faster than regular bottles. The market for them is primarily the restaurant trade and the resale value of two halves rarely equals a whole.

Rule Number Eight: Buy some futures.

Some IGW, especially in good years, is only available as futures. Buying futures means that you contract with your wine merchant to pay for cases of wine that will be delivered to you at some point in the future, usually one or two years from the time of the contract. Futures offer special opportunities and special risks, which I discuss in Chapter Five; for the moment, just remember that if you want to buy #1 IGW, then you may have to commit yourself to buying it as futures.

Rule Number Nine: Keep a cellar log.

Keep a complete a log of your wines. The log should include the following:

When and where you bought your wines, including receipts

The purchase price

Provenance, for wines with previous owners

Tasting notes

A record of futures purchases, including the scheduled date of delivery

Location of the wine in your cellar

Obviously, it's not convenient to keep all this information literally in a single log; however, all of the information should be within easy reach. The information associated with a beginner's cellar is easily recollected. Most of my clients recall exactly when they bought their first case of wine, including where they bought it and how much they paid. Very few can answer the same questions for the twentieth or hundredth case. Even a modest investment in wine every year will soon build into a substantial cellar, making the last requirement critical, especially for insurance purposes. William F. Buckley, Jr., a good client, lost the labels on hundreds of bottles of wine when a storm flooded his cellar. Unfortunately he hadn't recorded the location of each of his wines so he was suddenly confronted with a cellar of anonymous Bordeaux. He could say with certainty that he owned Lafite and Lynch-Bages, but he'd be damned if he knew where to find them. The only way he could find out what he had was to check the wine and vintage named on the corks of the bottles.

Rule Number Ten: Do your homework.

Don't buy blindly. Wine homework means taking the trouble to inform yourself. In Chapter Three I detailed the different sources, printed and otherwise, that will expand your wine knowledge. Use them! Develop a relationship with an informed merchant; look at wine texts; take a tasting class or join a wine club; introduce yourself to other wine buyers with experience in investing. Find the local grapevine and utilize it.

One of the most difficult problems for the novice wine buyer is learning to assess the value of information. Don't depend exclusively on a single merchant or isolated newsletter for your information; aside from the possibility that they may be wrong, slavish adherence to someone else's attitudes about wine will never allow your own preferences and inclinations to develop. Once you begin to look for information, a dozen experts will pop up (including myself) to tell you what to do. However, you would do better to educate yourself about the winemaking process, and then follow your instincts after that.

Homework also means making the necessary inquiries to your state liquor authorities to learn about your local laws. (Are permits necessary for the transportation of wine in and out of your state? Under what circumstances can you sell your wine?) An appendix in the back of this book lists the addresses and telephone numbers for alcohol and beverage authorities in all fifty states.

DIVERSITY

No broker puts all his chips on one stock and no wine lover worth his salt will either. Diversity is not simply a rule, it represents an attitude toward your entire investment, a commitment to expand your range beyond what is easy or familiar.

Rule Number Eleven: Diversify.

Speculators disagree with this rule, preferring to concentrate their money on one or two big names and then to let their investment ride. This isn't practical for the smaller wine buyer for several reasons: there are limited quantities of the top IGW, and they tend to go first to the volume buyer; second, it's boring, especially if you can't drink your investment for a decade or more; and third, market conditions change, making straight purchases of the most recent vintage IGW imprudent.

Break up your investment. The various categories of IGW provide not only a range in risk, but a range in price. Don't become addicted to the upper levels of IGW simply because those contain the most impressive names. Sometimes the price gap between the first ten wines and the next twenty is astounding, just as the price gap between Pétrus and even the other top-ranked growths can be breathtaking.

The top wines always command top dollar; the slightly less famous have almost the same degree of quality and longevity, but they cost substantially less. For example, during 1986, 1982 Mouton-Rothschild sold for $81 per bottle at some stores. It is without a doubt one of the most famous wines in history. At the same time, the 1982 Gruaud-Larose, a second-growth, was selling for $30, and 1982 Rausan-Ségla could be had for $15. Even among the top one percent of wines few names possess the fame of a Mouton-Rothschild, but that doesn't negate their value as investments. Buy them.

Bordeaux, the classic IGW, is only one area of investment. Spread your risk among investment-grade Ports and California IGW as well. You can still preserve your security while venturing afield from France, since these wines meet the criteria for IGW.

Rule Number Twelve: Buy different vintages.

Spreading your investment through several different vintages helps insulate you from the effects of speculation fever in any given year. Also, as prices of recent superior vintages of a wine tend to rise, they tend to pull up previous years of the same wine—although not necessarily at the same time. The quickest price fluctuations around a given wine occur within a year or two of the vintage as everybody scrambles to get in on the action; then the price seems to remain dormant for a few years.

Older vintages of the same wine often seem to rise when the most recent vintages are in a lull. Also, the older the vintage, the greater its security against the ravages of the market. The prices for 1982 and 1983 IGW will respond quicker to market pressure because there are more of them available for buying and selling. Earlier vintages of the same wines experience a more steady climb.

Robert Parker, Jr., suggests that wine lovers interested in Port buy older vintages exclusively. Because Port is the longest-lived of all categories of IGW, quite commonly lasting fifty or a hundred years, he notes that while recent vintages of Port are inexpensive, you have to wait for ten years to see any significant movement in the price. If you're as old as I am, or you're not considering passing your cellar on to your children, you might want to consider his advice.

TIMING

The wine trade, like any other investment market, has its cycles of high and low prices. Awareness and anticipation of these cycles will help you buy and sell your IGW at the most advantageous moments. Unfortunately, as in the stock market, there are no guaranteed formulas to predict the exact instant of the peak of a boom market or when a long decline is about to turn upward. However, as in the stock market, there is always an ample supply of gossip, rumor and genuine hard information bruited about. As you avail yourself of some of my suggestions on how to get information you should become more adept at separating the wheat from the chaff. Try to gauge current interest in, and prices of, wine by the articles you read, the talk you hear, the general word on wine that seems to be around. In other words, keep your ear to the ground. Beyond that, here are some basic rules to consider.

Rule Number Thirteen: Think of your investments over the long term.

Bide your time; wine investing is a long-range commitment. Occasionally, as with the 1982s, you can buy a case for $200 and sell it one year later for $800, but this is not typical. Usually you have to keep your wine for at least four years to show any return, and the highest returns, with the exception of a few superstar wines, come to those wine lovers willing to wait between eight and twenty years.

The scarcer a wine becomes, the more its value increases. As time passes, the number of remaining bottles in a vintage shrinks and even inferior vintages make remarkable gains in price. For example, 1977 Lafite costs $90 per bottle at the Golden Nugget Casino in Atlantic City. This poor vintage probably cost the Golden Nugget $10 per bottle in 1980. This just might top the casino's return on baccarat or roulette.

George M. Schofield is a financial planner who works primarily with the wine trade. In 1985 he researched the price histories of 300 California Cabernets, reserve and non-reserve, produced in twenty-six "premium" wineries. He estimated original prices from periodicals and winery records; for present prices he surveyed seventeen different stores located in San Francisco, Napa Valley and New York City. The survey included data from wines dating back as far as 1957, but concentrated on the vintages from 1970 through 1982. Among the results of his survey, he discovered that wine appreciates at different rates, depending on its age. The results are as follows:

> 1–4   years = little or no return
> 5–7   years = 11.98% return
> 8–20 years = 21.34% return
> 21–25 years = 16.10% return

As Figure 1 demonstrates, the average return for wines five to twenty-five years old was just under twenty percent. (He attributed the decline after twenty years to concern over the aging potential of wines and the increased necessity for proper maintenance—correct storage, recorking, and so forth.) Mr. Schofield went on to cite other surveys, particularly of prices at the Heublein auction. During the thirteen-year period of

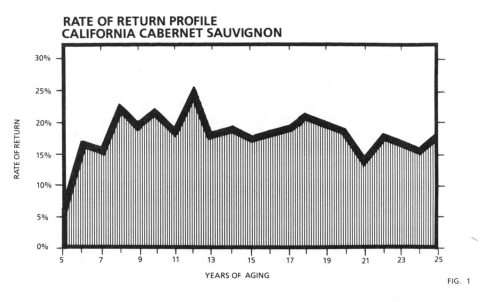

**RATE OF RETURN PROFILE
CALIFORNIA CABERNET SAUVIGNON**

RATE OF RETURN

YEARS OF AGING

FIG. 1

the survey Bordeaux prices rose at an annual rate of almost twenty-three percent.

Clearly, it pays to buy and wait.

Develop your portfolio of fine wine with the same patience you give to other long-range investments—with an eye to your distant future and that of your children.

Rule Number Fourteen: Watch for market breaks.

Market breaks are periods when prices head downward, sometimes precipitously. In the two and a half decades of America's involvement with fine wine there have been two major market breaks, the first from 1962 to 1963; the second from 1973 to 1974. Market breaks represent periods of opportunity and danger; they occur in all areas of collectibles and serve as correctives to overinflated prices.

Since this book isn't concerned with teaching you to become an adept short-term speculator there are only two pieces of advice you need to know concerning market breaks:

Don't allow panic at falling prices to force you into selling your wine; markets always recover and prices eventually rebound.

Secondly, market breaks make lots of good IGW available at bargain prices, usually from frightened speculators who begin to sense a bursting bubble and as a consequence dump their wine onto a saturated market.

The major breaks in the American market have been preceded by price increases (not unlike the ones of the present day). I remember the period right before the sixties' break. Prices for the 1961 vintage were going through the roof. Expensive wines of the period ($3.99/bottle) suddenly cost $7 or $8, the equivalent of $50 or $60 at today's prices. When second growths shattered the $5 mark I thought the market was going insane.

Then in 1962 and 1963 the wine market took a swan dive that looked like it would never end. The price for a case of 1961 Lafite tumbled from $120 to $80 per case in three months (plus a ten-percent discount if you paid your bill within forty-eight hours). Because I was just a budding wine lover in 1962, and not a keenly aware, hardheaded realist, I didn't buy any 1961 Lafite. Today those cases are worth $4,000–$5,000 each. It pains me still.

High prices also heralded the 1973–74 break. A case of 1966 Pétrus half-bottles shot up to $1,500, then dropped within a couple of months to $700. The seventies' break showed what happens when people buy blindly; the psychological optimism of 1970–73 lured speculators into the market who bid up the prices of 1971s (an inconsistent vintage) and 1972s (a dreadful one, but even more expensive than 1971) without asking themselves if the wines were really worth it. In April of 1973 a friend of mine bought one hundred cases of Brane-Cantenac for $112 a case; the price began to drop almost immediately. Instead of battening down the hatches, he desperately began seeking a buyer.

Three months later he unloaded the wine—for $22 a case.

In December 1986 the market for red Burgundies experienced a break; I suspect that the market for red Bordeaux will follow in 1987. The prices for recent Bordeaux vintages have escalated without any sign of the market rebelling. I advise you to hang on to your previous purchases and keep your eyes open for steals.

Rule Number Fifteen: Don't buy in times of excessively high prices.

How, you ask, am I supposed to know when prices are out of line?

Clive Coates, the esteemed British wine writer and critic, suggests you compare opening prices for new vintages with present prices for the last superior vintage. The two should be roughly equivalent.

Another way is to ask your wine merchant. Simply because you call a temporary halt to your IGW purchases of the most recent vintage doesn't mean that you've stopped buying wine altogether, and any merchant who's willing to sell you expensive wine ought to have the courage to tell you when it's *too* expensive.

Twice in the last two decades—in 1971 and in 1983—I've told my clients that prices for French IGW were too high and that they ought to shift their wine dollars into other areas of IGW. The effects of inflation prompted the first instance; speculation, the second.

Wine, like other commodities, increases in value with inflation. In 1971 I made a trip to France for the express purpose of sitting down with Bordeaux shippers and suppliers. We needed a strategy to cope with the runaway inflation for Bordeaux wines then plaguing the American market (an ambitious task, I admit, but we vintners are always willing to try). In 1970 America was the major export market for Bordeaux. Sales of these wines to America had doubled between 1969 and 1970 (almost a third of all the wines sold in America were French). The demand for the relatively meager supply of French wine-pushed prices to astronomical levels. I felt that unless something was done to halt the price spiral, Bordeaux would soon become unreasonably expensive, thus pricing itself out of the market. In fact, as a result of the French trade's refusal to confront the problem, that is precisely what happened.

By the end of 1971, I was recommending that investors pass over Bordeaux. The price had inflated beyond reason. I suggested lesser-known names and brands, wines still priced under $100 per case.

In 1983 I again warned my clients about wine prices. The 1982s did not then (and do not today) seem like worthwhile investments.

Remember, if a wine's purchase price is so high that it cannot reasonably increase over the coming years, it's not IGW. The principle holds true regardless of the reason for the increase; whether inflation, as was the case in 1971, or speculative fever, as in 1983.

THE FINAL RULE

Your investments should pay for your drinking wines. Make it happen.

CHAPTER FIVE

WINE FUTURES

The wine lover who can never seem to find a merchant with a case or two of the investment-grade wine he needs may want to consider wine futures. Bordeaux has a time-honored history of contracting for the sale of its wine in advance of bottling. In the eighteenth century English merchants often purchased wine *en primeur,* that is, still in the barrels. The merchants then bottled it themselves for the retail market. In times when wine has been in high demand, growers anxious to lock in a high price have often sold their product *sur souche,* while the grapes were still on the vine. Growers were sometimes more reckless than shrewd. If the harvest wasn't as large as anticipated a grower could find himself contractually obliged to supply more wine than the vineyard could provide. Bankruptcy was the result. Many Bordeaux estates have changed hands as a result of such cockiness or miscalculation.

The modern wine futures contract resembles a purchase in the commodities market (without quite as much risk); you buy a contract for wine that will be delivered to you at a future date, usually eighteen to twenty-four months after what is known as the first futures offering. Typically, you have an oral agreement with your wine merchant; the usual terms require full payment of the futures price at the time of the offering. When you buy futures, you are purchasing wine at below the eventual market price—you hope. You're taking a calculated risk, based upon the wine's history, reputation, and the publicity surrounding the particular vintage. If all goes well you get your wine a couple of years down the road at a considerable savings over the buyers who waited until the bottles actually arrived in a merchant's shop. If you purchase a case of wine at the futures price of $100 and in the months before delivery the price of the wine rises to $300, you have obviously done well. You can either drink the wine which you obtained at bargain prices or you can sell it for a handsome profit. The advantage for the wine merchant is that he can use your money for about two and a half years, interest-free; it provides cash flow into his business.

As a rule, the first futures offerings for Bordeaux wines appear in

April to June of the year following the vintage. Depending on the strategy of the château and the activity in the market, a second offering may follow the first. The first offering appears in the spring because its price is usually pegged to the official opening price of the vintage; traditionally (although not always), the individual châteaux announce their openings in March. The 1986 vintage, to take the most recent case, will probably become widely available as futures between April and June of 1987. The actual cases of wine will arrive between June and October of 1989.

The overwhelming majority of wines are never sold as futures. The futures market tends to exclude most wines except top-flight Bordeaux. The fabulous coups of those who bought Bordeaux futures in the early sixties has entrenched these wines in the hearts and minds of many would-be buyers, although you can now find futures for Port and Burgundy, for German and Italian wines and for vintage French champagne. One of the first futures offerings ever made for an American wine was by Robert Mondavi of California on his 1982 Reserve Cabernet Sauvignon. The offering was actually a "short future," meaning that the time between the offering and the delivery was only nine months. The offering, made in March 1986, was $235 per case or $1,175 per five cases. The wine was delivered in October 1986, by which time it had risen to over $290 per case. I tasted this wine in 1985, and I believe it has the thirty-to-forty-year staying power you should expect from an investment wine. Wine lovers who lack the discipline to wait that long will find the wine quite good right now, still in its infancy.

The primary selling point of futures is that they guarantee you access to wine which may be unavailable at a later date. At the very least, when you buy futures you almost automatically guarantee yourself a bargain, as well as give yourself a shot at a fabulous profit. The price of the wine at the time of delivery is rarely lower than its futures price.

After the first offering, futures prices can increase just as regular bottle prices increase. In the months after a harvest more and more information becomes available about the quality of the wine; wine writers publish tasting comments and updates in newsletters and magazines, all contributing to the reputation of the vintage. A vintage's reputation, for good or ill, spreads throughout the wine world as the year goes on.

In good years, dealers raise their futures prices as the months progress. A superior vintage receives confirmation as more tasting information makes its way back from France; the later the tastings, the more accurate (and possibly favorable) the picture of the wine. Futures prices soar for good wine in good years; the regular bottle prices increase over time as the wine becomes scarcer and its reputation expands further.

Let's examine some recent futures offerings. In early 1983, when futures sales of 1982 wines began, you could have purchased futures for a case of Pétrus for $600. That was the highest any wine ever opened on the futures market. Two years later, in 1985, that case sold for $2,500. In 1984, Sherry-Lehmann, the well-known New York wine merchant, featured 1983 Léoville-Las-Cases futures in their catalogue at $220 per case, $18.33 a bottle; in June of 1986 it was $640 per case. 1982 Mouton-Rothschild opened for futures sales at $300 per case in January 1983; on April 1, 1986, the quote for the same case was $900–$1,000. The wine had tripled in value.

More importantly, by April 1, 1986, there was little 1982 Pétrus, 1982 Mouton, or any other top IGW Bordeaux from the 1982 vintage available, except at even higher prices. People who bought futures were buying insurance against just this possibility.

HOW TO LOSE MONEY IN THE FUTURES MARKET

If you take care to buy your futures from a reputable merchant, there's only one way to lose money in the futures market: buying futures in a bad year. I didn't offer futures on the 1984 vintage. Sherry-Lehmann, one of the largest futures vendors in New York, offered a very limited list. As a wine buyer with an eye to investment, you shouldn't buy futures in poor vintages for the same reasons you shouldn't buy bottles from the same year; the investment potential is nil.

In good years, buy #1 and #2 IGW as futures. Stay away from the others. The opening prices of IGW wines inevitably seem to rise every year, except in times of absolute disaster. Even the mediocre 1984 vintage opened higher than the superb 1983. The investment potential of the 1984s is minuscule, but the French have an interest in preserving the price and prestige of their wines. In bad years, price increases are attributed to small vintages, increased labor costs and the higher price of pesticides to control rot. In good years, the price goes up because the wine is in demand. You may have also noticed French wine prices keep going up, no matter what the relationship between the dollar and the franc. For the moment, the dollar is weakening against the franc. We expect prices to rise, but a year and a half ago, the reverse was true. In the beginning of 1985, 1982 Mouton Rothschild went from $450 per case to $700. This was while the franc was sinking from 9.50 to 10.50. This should have meant a reduction in price (dollars buy more francs, so the wine, priced in francs, should be cheaper); but supply and demand and greed were hard at work, therefore you got your Mouton for $700. By December 1986, 1982 Mouton cost $1,200 per case.

Poor vintages, despite their opening prices, do not appreciate. Regarding futures, stick to the straight and narrow: buy IGW wine in good years.

THE IMPORTANCE OF A MERCHANT

People may lose money in futures because they've made a poor choice of a wine merchant. A knowledgeable, experienced wine merchant is your assurance that you won't encounter the chief difficulties with futures purchases—wines that aren't available and nondelivery of your wines.

Your contract is only as good as your merchant. How do you know you will receive your wine? A contract exists between you and a wine merchant. Would it hold up in court? Currently, there's scant legal precedent and no regulation in the area of wine futures. If a sufficient number of merchants default on their deliveries, the courts and state legislatures will undoubtedly become involved. To date, this hasn't occurred, which is why the selection of a merchant is doubly important.

Aside from providing you with the latest information available from the trade grapevine regarding your intended purchases, the merchant's experience assures you access to the futures offerings of the most desirable estates. The top thirty red Bordeaux wines are enormously popular, with wine lovers and speculators alike. The highest return on futures purchases often occurs with those châteaux whose output is less than five thousand cases; Pétrus, Ausone and La Grave-Trigant-de-Boisset, for example. The figures below are for the 1983 vintage.

	MARCH 1985	FEBRUARY 1987
Pétrus	$795	$1,500
Ausone	590	1,400
La Grave	90	265

Scarcity, once again. The more a vintage's quality begins to unfold, the more its finiteness comes into play. A good merchant will not only have access to these wines, but he will have an exact idea of how many cases he can sell with a certainty that he'll deliver. That wine buyers are concerned about access to these wines in good vintages is evidenced in my own sales figures. Almost sixty-five percent of my futures sales of 1985s were to out-of-state customers. Some of these sales involved a great deal of inconvenience to the client, what with having to acquire the requisite permits from the alcohol and beverage authorities of their home states before I could legally ship their wine. These people know their wines and when they want them.

A qualified merchant protects his clients against nondelivery, another bugaboo in the futures market. Shippers have shorted cases in my consignments. One whole shipment, direct from a château, disappeared altogether. An examination of the shipping documents, sent to me from France, showed the ship's registry as South Molucca. Someone had a hell of a party at my expense. On another occasion a salesman from an unfamiliar wholesaler talked me into using his boss as my supplier for my futures sales. I paid the company thirty percent of the total value of my order. When the 1982 futures prices began escalating, the owner of the wholesale business decided he wouldn't make enough profit. He fired his salesman and denied I'd ever contracted for the wine.

These incidents meant that some of my futures clients would not have received their Léoville-Las-Cases and Cos d'Estournel if I hadn't found other sources (at practically triple my original wholesale price). As a discerning futures buyer, it pays to investiage the delivery record of the merchant with whom you're contemplating doing business.

Before the 1982 vintage, the futures part of my business was a neat, elegant sidelight to our main concern, selling the wine already in stock. But the incredible hype from wine writers after the first barrel tastings blew the market wide open. Our futures business doubled in a single year. The pressure on an inexperienced merchant who wants to stay competitive, but has no experience in the futures market, is incredible, increasing the chances of mismanaged logistics. In 1983, as word of the quality of the 1982 vintage became known, a buying panic spread across the United States, infecting investors who couldn't tell the difference between a Bordeaux and a Barolo. Some, without checking their merchant's credentials, blindly sent off money for wines which never appeared in the United States. I've heard several stories of wine buyers who were burned on the 1982s in New York alone. The merchants were inexperienced and relatively small—each merchant's futures sales only amounted to between fifty and a hundred cases. Unfortunately, they didn't anticipate that prices would double or triple by delivery time. They spent the money, assuming they'd be able to get the wine from their wholesalers as the delivery date approached.

They were wrong.

Look for a wine dealer who has a long track record of on-time delivery to futures clients, a history of dealing with producers and who knows just how many cases he can expect.

SPECULATORS

Speculators, buying in fifty- and one-hundred-case lots, purchase enormous amounts of hard-to-get wine futures, the ones on the #1 IGW list. By delivery time the wines are sold out or available only at astronomical prices. Wine is not a commodity that can be generated by simply starting up production again. Once the vintage is off the vines and into the bottles, that's all she wrote. In the meantime, the price has risen from $600 to $2,400 per case.

The overblown 1982 vintage is an example of speculative power, of investors waiting for a big kill. I know of one such person who can't wait to offer his 1982 Pétrus for $5,000 per case when the time comes that buyers are starving for Pétrus; his secret wish is to raise the price to $10,000.

If there was an impression of camaraderie among members of the wine trade, the 1982 vintage certainly exposed where it existed and where it did not. Before 1982, a merchant who got into trouble with futures could always plead his case with the château, hoping for an extra allotment of wine. I personally know of a merchant who ended up in the unenviable position of owing a client a hundred cases of Pétrus. The futures purchase was $60,000; the worth of the wine at time of delivery was $300,000. The client, who is also known to me as a canny investor, sent the merchant a letter offering to simply take the money instead of the wine. Generous terms. The wine dealer desperately called everybody in the trade who owed him a favor; he managed to locate a total of fifteen cases of uncommitted Pétrus.

He's still in business today, but God only knows what sort of deal he cut with the devil to extricate himself.

A vintage that causes a lot of speculative activity poses an additional danger to wine buyers in that it attracts all sorts of con men and confidence tricksters. Desperate buyers will listen to anyone who claims he has access to unobtainable wines. A Swiss group sold many millions of dollars' worth of the 1982 Bordeaux and then disappeared before making delivery. In Chicago, a wine merchant paid $1.5 million to a wholesaler and his clients never saw their wine. He was the victim of an unscrupulous Frenchman who went around the U.S. collecting money for wines he had no intention of delivering. In San Francisco a wine shop closed after receiving $100,000 of futures sales on which delivery proved impossible.

Lawsuits offer a remedy (the San Francisco clients recouped some of their loss by suing the importer, whom the bankrupt merchant had already paid for their wines). But legal action isn't practical most of the time. The best defense against such an occurrence is to thoroughly check the reputation of your merchant. Ask for the names of other clients who've bought futures from him and ask the opinion of other futures investors.

Imagine spending $800 on futures for three cases of wine. Now suppose your futures selection turns out to be particularly astute; as the months pass you see the value of your wine rise to $2,000. As the delivery date approaches you eagerly cross the days off your calendar. Finally, the happy morning arrives. But much to your chagrin, your merchant explains that he goofed up your order; your wine, much to his regret, isn't available. What would you do? Would you be content if he simply offered to refund your $800? Wouldn't you want the market value of your wine? At present, nothing obligates merchants to pay the market value of the wine, except their interest in assuaging a justifiably disgruntled customer. I believe that question will have to be settled in court, hopefully soon.

In the meantime, be sure to get a written statement of the merchant's policy regarding nondeliverable wines. Get a guarantee that should wine not be delivered, you will be paid fair market value established by current retail or wholesale lists. Keep accurate records, with receipts, of all your futures purchases.

All merchants may experience a shortage of wines for reasons beyond their control. What's important is that you find a trustworthy merchant who knows the market and will indemnify you. When a wholesaler left me unable to deliver two cases of 1982 Certan de May, I offered my client two options: I would guarantee to obtain the wine for him at a later date (not a bad deal, since he wouldn't have to worry about storing it in the interim) or I'd pay him the market value of his purchase. The second option, though justified, is not standard practice. He opted for the money. I wrote him a check for $1,500, no questions asked.

EARLY BIRDS—HOW TO GET THE WINE YOU WANT

Until the next market hiccup, we're probably going to have to learn to live with speculators gobbling up the choicest futures whenever they get the chance. We live in a world dominated by PR; the right financing, the right advertising and the right celebrity spokesperson can sell anything. A raft of newsletters and columnists spew out reams of information for anyone willing to pause long enough to read it. The hope for sudden wealth is seducing more people into the wine market than ever, a trend that will continue as long as prices continue to rise. The market for 1982s vividly illustrates this; more than any other factor, it was the glut of American buyers which propelled Bordeaux prices upward. The question then becomes, How can you get the investment-grade wine you want?

I have a solution: early bird futures.

In early February of 1986 I offered futures on the 1985 vintage of the top vineyards before the châteaux themselves had announced their opening prices. I announced my own prices and I collected down payments of fifty percent from anyone who wanted to buy these futures.

Other merchants criticized me for selling futures at "fantasy prices."

The traditional futures offering by your local wine merchant is the sum of several figures: the opening prices announced by the château, plus various percentages for those who facilitate the movement of the wine from France to the United States; these may include a broker, a négociant, a shipper, an importer (who probably gets the biggest chunk) and then final percentages for the wholesaler and retailer. The futures price is between double and triple the estate's opening price.

Bordeaux vineyards customarily announce their opening prices in April. Yet here I was taking money for wines whose prices hadn't even been officially established yet. Other merchants intended to sell 1985 futures, but they certainly weren't taking anyone's money yet—not until they knew the price of the wine. I was rolling the dice based on my experience in the Bordeaux market, which I felt allowed me to predict the opening prices, and I was guaranteeing my clients access to the wine at a certain price.

If I had been wrong and the "official" prices were lower than I charged, I would have brewed trouble in wine paradise, in the form of clients who felt they were overpaying. If my predictions equaled official prices, at least no one would lose any money. And if my prices were lower than official rates, my clients would be the toast of the town, as beneficiaries of the best deal around.

My prices, as things transpired, were lower.

In some respects, the prestige of the châteaux involved made it a foolproof operation. Let's use Château Lafite as an illustration. In order to calculate my early bird price for Lafite I began doing some research. In late December I spoke to the importer of Lafite and asked him to estimate Lafite's opening price. Usually châteaux don't release opening prices until April, so both of us were speculating. We listened to each other's observations about the wine market and we discussed the dollar-franc relationship. Eventually we agreed the futures price for Lafite could could go as high as $700–$800.

Armed with this figure, I called friends in England. Christie's of London provided me with a range of auction figures for the years 1982 and 1983. In 1982, the 1966 Lafite sold for $780–$930 per case, and the 1970 Lafite went for $690–$780 per case. One year later, auctioneers were selling the same wines for $1,380–$1,725 and $960–$1,110, increases of roughly seventy percent and forty percent! English friends in the wine trade informed me that early reports from France were heralding the 1985s as a spectacular vintage, that barring some catastrophic error in the blending, the wine would easily equal, and quite possibly surpass, the 1966s and 1970s.

I reached two conclusions. First of all, the 1985 Lafite would appreciate faster and higher than the 1966s and 1970s. *Investors would make money on this wine regardless of what they paid at opening.* If my Lafite futures turned out to be a shade higher than the official futures, it really wouldn't matter; investors would still earn a substantial gain. Secondly, with earlier great vintages of Lafite doing so well on the auction market it made sense that if the château anticipated another good vintage on the way, they'd raise their opening price by at least the percentage of the previous year's appreciation, in this case at least forty percent.

I had to look up the opening price on 1984 Lafite—$400 per case—since I hadn't sold any futures the previous year. An additional forty percent pushed the price up to $480; after calculating percentages for the various middlemen, I arrived at $560. So now I had a range of $560–$700. I wanted to offer clients a deal they couldn't refuse, but I wanted to do it without putting myself out of business. I split the difference and settled on $630, my early bird futures price for 1985 Lafite. Since the first reaction to my "unofficial" futures offering was sluggish I lowered the price to $595.

Lafite futures officially opened, several months later, at $630. My clients got a bargain.

I performed the same sort of torturous calculations with Mouton-Rothschild and Margaux. The message seemed clear: prices of prestige wines in good years—a designation the trade was predicting for the 1985 vintage—were not going to drop. There could be hiccups or blips, but prices eventually firmed.

I offered 1985 Mouton and 1985 Margaux for $590 per case. In all, I listed twenty-five key wines, all the first-growths plus the next fifteen difficult-to-get vineyards. I shaved some money off my cost by going directly to some of the châteaux and paying them up front for their wine, thus eliminating much of the importer's finance charge. When other merchants finally posted their own futures prices I found I was either selling wine for the same price or lower on all but two vineyards. My clients were guaranteed their wine, and they received it at a highly competitive rate.

Not bad for a merchant who was making up fantasy prices.

A FUTURES PORTFOLIO

Let's consider a hypothetical investment of just over $20,000 in 1985 futures, purchased in early 1986. I recommend, if purchasing in large amounts, that you diversify and take several cases from different châteaux.

5 cases Mouton-Rothschild at $600 each	$3,000
5 cases Lafite-Rothschild at $630 each	3,150
5 cases Latour at $600 each	3,000
5 cases Haut-Brion at $500 each	2,500
5 cases Cheval Blanc at $600 each	3,000
5 cases La Grave-Trigant-de-Boisset at $250 each	1,250
5 cases Margaux at $600 each	3,000
1 case Pétrus at $1,200	1,200
TOTAL	$20,100

The combined production of all eight of the châteaux in this portfolio is slightly more than 100,000 cases annually. Perhaps 10,000 cases
will reach the U.S. during the first offering, with another 15,000 arriving with later price increases. The portfolio includes one newcomer and
seven veterans, all known for scarcity. This type of approach gives you
a nice mix without taking colossal risks.

You might wonder why only one case of Pétrus appears in this hypothetical portfolio. Why not ten cases, since it commands such high
resale and has such long life? The answer is the scarce supply of Pétrus.
You might be lucky to get even one case of it. You'll notice one unknown name on the list, La Grave-Trigant-de-Boisset. Why not take a
chance on a good-looking newcomer, as part of a futures package? La
Grave's production is slightly over 2,000 cases per year, so it's rare.

The suggested list includes five cases each of Mouton, Lafite, Latour, Haut-Brion, Cheval Blanc and Margaux, normally a tall order at
these prices. *Unless you acted early.* At the second futures offering, nine
months to a year after the first official offering, these prices will probably rise about twenty-five percent. Increase naturally depends upon the
progress of the first futures offering. In the event that buyers snap up
the first offerings, Bordeaux owners will promptly raise prices for the
second. The 1983 futures had second offering prices about twenty percent higher across the board than the first offering, just nine months
later. That this could happen, even after the fierce speculation in 1982s
had literally drained investment resources out of the market, is a testa-
ment to these wines' enduring popularity with investors. In January
1987 a predictable dip occurred in 1983 Bordeaux prices. This correction lasted six weeks—an opportunity for the nimble-footed.

In summary, my advice concerning futures investment centers around
five basic rules:

Rule Number 1. Use a reliable wine merchant, one with a history
of dealing with producers and wholesalers, and who knows what he can
realistically expect for his allotment of wines. Check his track record
regarding delivery. If it seems at all shaky, look for another merchant.
Ask for a written statement regarding his policy on undelivered wine.
Will he offer an alternative wine of the same vintage? The original
wine at a later date? Or a cash refund of your futures, at present market
value?

Rule Number 2. Keep accurate records of purchases, with receipts
that document your delivery times.

Rule Number 3. Try to negotiate a partial down payment. If your
purchase is over $5,000 I recommend a down payment of twenty per-
cent to thirty percent. Whenever and wherever possible, pay as little
as necessary up front.

Rule Number 4. Shop for early bird futures. I understand that merchants in California and Chicago will soon begin offering their own early futures.

Rule Number 5. Buy futures as you would bottled wine: good wine in good years.

And watch out for Moluccan cargo ships.

CHAPTER SIX

SAMPLE WINE PORTFOLIOS

Putting together a wine portfolio is a lot like buying a new suit of clothes: much depends on whether you want to stand out in a crowd and on how much you want to spend. The following portfolios take a conservative approach, emphasizing #1 investment-grade wine whenever possible. Diversity is another matter altogether. Wine cellars grow and change character after several years of devotion; one season's passion for Pauillac may redirect itself to Pomerol, especially in vintages of unequal quality. The flamboyant wine lover who takes pride in his cellar display of double magnums will spend his investment dollars differently than a scholarly specialist whose Ports mature undisturbed in a warehouse locker.

The portfolios in this chapter were assembled from wines easily obtained in the New York retail market. They reflect prices current at some point in 1986 or, in the case of wines not yet released, on their likely prices when the vineyards make the wine available. My assumption, in the latter case, is that you won't spend all of your investment at one time, in a single purchase. You may buy futures (marked as such) at one point in the year; in other circumstances you may want to pick up a case or two of a new release that's just hit the shelves.

$2,200 PORTFOLIO

	1986	1991 (EST.)
1 case Lafite 1985 (futures)	$650	1,200
1 case Lynch-Bages 1985 (futures)	275	650
1 case Mondavi Reserve Cabernet Sauvignon 1982 (futures)	250	550
1 case Côte Rôtie 1983 (Guigal)	250	500
1 case Graham Port 1983	300	900
Assorted duplicate bottles	475	

Portfolio Analysis: At this level you're pretty much restricted to just covering the basics. Unfortunately $2,000 is not the investment it was five years ago; your options have shrunk. My choices are pretty conservative, with an aim to providing a secure starter investment for neophyte wine lovers.

All portfolios ought to contain at least one blue-chip stock, and Lafite is the IBM of Bordeaux wines. Lafite may be the most recognized aristocratic wine in the world. Its history of trading at ever-increasing prices and the public's unshakable belief in its value make it a good foundation for a beginning portfolio.

Lynch-Bages gets my vote as the poor man's Lafite. Its fifth-growth ranking in the Médoc classification of 1855 is a good example of how things can change in one century. André Cazes, mayor of Pauillac, manages the vineyard with a consistent eye for quality, a role he inherited from his father, Jean-Charles Cazes, who established the wine's reputation in the fifties.

I harangued Robert Mondavi for fifteen years to sell his Cabernets as futures. Last year he finally acquiesced. Mondavi's participation in futures is significant because it represents the stamp of approval from the California wine establishment. Undoubtedly many other California winemakers will follow his lead. His 1982 Reserve Cabernet is particularly striking, structured much like the 1983 Bordeaux wines, but with an overwhelming mouthful of fruit for such a tannic wine. This wine will last for at least thirty years, maybe longer. Mondavi wines not only have good distribution, but the winery maintains a high profile. It seems quite likely that this wine could be worth $800–$900 in ten years.

Côte Rôtie combines the finesse of a Bordeaux wine with the power of a Rhône. The firm of Guigal cares enough about their wines to avoid filtration and fining, producing wines with backbone intended for laying down. Guigal has become legendary in the last ten years, not only for producing wines, but also for marketing them. He's the number one Rhône producer. His Côte Rôtie and Hermitage are famous for their longevity. The lesser wines (Gigondas, Côtes-du-Rhône) tend to be shorter lived. I chose the Côte Rôtie so that someone with even a modest investment could see how to move away from the traditional IGW route.

The prices of most True Vintage Ports move closely together. 1983 was the most recently declared vintage. Since the prices of many Ports almost doubled in 1986 it would be an oversight not to include at least one case here, even if it won't be drinkable for a good fifteen years.

The assorted extra bottles provide you with a range of tasting opportunity, as a means of seeing how your wines are aging, and also as a stopgap against breaking into the cases themselves. If you only have one case of a particular wine, it takes incredible fortitude to resist the desire to "try a Lafite, just this once." Go ahead, give it a try, just don't compromise your investment in the process.

$5,000 PORTFOLIO

	1986	1991 (EST.)
1 case Margaux 1985 (futures)	$650	1,150
1 case La Grave-Trigant-de-Boisset 1985	250	590
1 case Montelena Cabernet Sauvignon 1984 (scheduled for release in the fall of 1987)	250	480
1 case Jordan Cabernet 1982	200	450
1 case La Tâche 1983	1200	1750
1 case Pichon-Lalande 1985 (futures)	400	690
1 case St. Jean Chardonnay, Robert Young Vineyard 1984 (scheduled for release in the summer of 1987)	250	450
1 case B.V. Georges de Latour Private Reserve Cabernet 1981	250	500
1 case Taylor 1983 Port	400	1000
2 cases Fonseca 1983 Port	530	1200
Assorted extra bottles	620	

Portfolio Analysis: With a slightly larger investment your portfolio can range considerably further afield; you have the freedom to develop more eclectic interests. To reflect this, I've selected a more daring range of wines, at both ends of the spectrum.

Margaux seemed to be riding on its fame in the sixties and early seventies, but in 1976 the château was sold to André Mentzelopoulos. The new owner showed a great commitment to restoring the vineyard, renovating the buildings and investing in new equipment. The 1978 vintage was superb and the 1979 was great as well (in a year with uneven results over the rest of Bordeaux).

La Grave-Trigant-de-Boisset, a wine I've had occasion to mention several times in the course of this book, is the long shot of the portfolio. La Grave certainly doesn't have the noble history of better-known châteaux, but its association with the Mouiex family (Christian, son of Jean-Pierre, is the proprietor) guarantees a commitment from people famous for producing and marketing luxury wines.

Montelena represents the apex of California cabernets. The winery itself was built in 1882, with the intention, if the original owners are to be believed, of making it the Lafite of California. My personal theory is that the winery's location in the foothills of Calistoga has contributed to its greatness. Like Lafite, which also sits back from the road, Montelena has been allowed to go about its business without too much distraction from the local hubbub of Napa. Its present fame originated with the 1973 Chardonnay, the winning entrant in a Paris tasting which included both established California Chardonnays and serious white Burgundies. Montelena has been out of the mainstream for a few years, but it seems to be coming back into popularity, especially since it's now generally available.

I've included Tom Jordan's wine because his vineyard is now over a decade old. His Cabernets have been fabulously successful (as he predicted they would be, to anyone who would listen). His master plan called for him to produce stylish, accessible wines in order to establish his name. Now that his reputation is solidly entrenched in the minds of California wine lovers I have a gut feeling he's beginning to produce long-lived wines. Starting with the 1979 I began noticing a slightly firmer structure to the wine, a trend that has continued through the most recent vintages. Keep your eyes peeled for reserve labels.

La Tâche is a step into the stratosphere of high-priced Burgundies. La Tâche would be the Lafite of Burgundy, except that Lafite only costs half as much and is usually easier to get. They do things the old way here; on one visit, I asked the winemaker about malolactic fermentation. His response was to give me a squint and ask, "What's that?" Nevertheless, the reputation of La Tâche is embedded in the stellar firmament and I can't foresee any circumstances that would dislodge it.

Mme. de Lencquesaing, director of the *societé civile* which owns Pichon-Lalande, has stated as her sole purpose the creation of legendary wine. She's as known for her demanding standards in the wine she produces as for her public fury with anyone who dares criticize it. She resides in the château, where she can keep a close watch on vineyard activity. I have nothing but superlatives to describe Pichon-Lalande. I tasted the 1980 vintage at the château against other second-growths and thought it was one of the best wines I'd ever tasted.

A Japanese company bought the Château St. Jean vineyard for $40 million a few years ago, a price that seemed excessive to me, but was perhaps a tribute to the efforts of St. Jean's winemaker, Richard Arrowwood. Certainly, I've always thought of it as special-occasion wine, with the equivalent in California prestige of a French wine like Corton-Charlemagne. Nineteen eighty-five was a watershed year for California wines. In my tasting experience these wines confirm the arrival of California as wine country with its own unique style, rather than as imitators of Bordeaux and Burgundy. Arrowwood, considered one of the best of his generation, has produced up to seven different Chardonnays in each vintage. Some of his best efforts have been released under the Robert Young label.

Beaulieu Vineyard's Georges de Latour Private Reserve Cabernet is a California benchmark. Along with the Heitz Martha's Vineyard and the Mondavi Cabernet Reserve, this wine declared unequivocally that California could produce superior wine. B.V. was founded in 1900 by Georges de Latour, who imported his cuttings from France; Andre Tchelistcheff was winemaker from 1937 until his retirement in 1973. Few California vineyards can claim to be as old as B.V. and fewer still can boast dedicated geniuses like Tchelistcheff. The continuity of a single, dedicated winemaker shines in a long succession of great vintages and in the immaculate state of the winery. I recommended the 1981 vintage because the vineyard holds their wines for five or six years before release; the 1985 will undoubtedly be a great wine, but won't be available for another three years.

Generally speaking, Taylor has commanded the highest prices of all the Vintage Ports in the last decade. It has a round, accessible style that lasts a long, long time. The 1983 probably won't be drinkable until almost 2000, and will probably continue improving for at least another fifty years.

Fonseca, by contrast, is more of a English-style Port, not quite as fat or accessible, and consequently without quite as wide an audience in the United States as the Taylor or Graham. It's made in an older style, like the Quinta da Noval. Port prices have increased faster than any other category of investment wine. Even these two, undrinkable for at least a decade, have risen sharply. Since June of 1986 the price for Taylor has risen over sixty-five percent; the Fonseca, by forty-seven percent. Presumably, this escalation will level off shortly, or the government will most likely switch from gold to Port as the desirable medium to back its currency.

$10,000 PORTFOLIO

	1986	1991 (EST.)
2 cases Ducru-Beaucaillou 1985 (futures)	$750	1,300
2 cases Palmer 1985 (futures)	800	1,550
2 cases Cos d'Estournel 1985 (futures)	700	1,450
2 cases Léoville-Las-Cases 1985 (futures)	800	1,500
1 case Haut-Brion red 1985 (futures)	600	900
1 case Haut-Brion white 1985 (futures)	500	1,000
2 cases Gaja Barbaresco 1985 (futures)	800	1,500
(Costa Russi or San Lorenzo, either will do)		
3 cases Cantemerle 1985	600	1,100
1 case d'Yquem 1980	700	1,200
3 cases Rutherford Ranch Napa Cabernet '82	400	800
(if available, otherwise 1983)		
1 case Corton-Charlemagne 1985 (futures)	400	650
(whichever is available: Bonneau de Martray,		
Joseph Drouhin or Louis Latour)		
1 case Richebourg 1983	1,100	1,650
2 cases Sandeman 1975 Port	400	700
Assorted extra bottles	1,000–1,500	

Portfolio Analysis: A $10,000 portfolio offers even more opportunity to diversify your investment. One of the problems I encounter among my clients is the tendency to sink all of their wine money into one or two easily recognized items. Aside from inducing an element of tedious sameness into their cellars (the all-my-friends-are-buying-Lafite syndrome), they're also passing up the chief joy of purchasing at this level: the chance to acquire something *truly rare*.

I picked Ducru-Beaucaillou right off the bat because I knew other selections in this portfolio might not be easily available. All things being equal, I was also inclined toward Léoville-Las-Cases, but my experience has been that Ducru is a shade easier to procure. The quality of both wines is absolutely first-rate, and both seem cheap to me, even at $400 a case. Monsieur Jean-Eugène Borie, who took over Ducru from his father, is a stickler for detail and a good trial-and-error person. The wines have consistently improved under his management. Ducru, Palmer, Las-Cases and Pichon-Lalande are thought of as similar in quality to Latour, despite their differences in the official classification. If Médoc were to reclassify its wines, undoubtedly these four would be promoted.

Château Palmer made its modern reputation with the 1961 vintage. In fact the estate itself was so impressed with the vintage, it ultimately bought much of it back. Palmer's classification as a third-growth doesn't reflect its true importance. Something else that impresses me about this wine—don't scoff—is the easy pronunciation of its name (after an English general who owned it in the nineteenth century). The estate of Palmer reminds me of California's Beaulieu Vineyard—the same atmosphere of meticulous continuity, of lives devoted to the care of wine and vineyards, permeates both establishments.

Cos d'Estournel was the first wine offered among 1985 futures. The Prats family, owners of the estate, opened with a low price, hoping thereby to set an example and thus keep a measure of sanity in Bordeaux prices. Their first offering reached the American market at $180 a case. Wine buyers gobbled it up at once. Other Bordeaux vineyards, responding less to the Prats' example than the enthusiasm of the American market, set their own opening prices at around $300 a case. Although Cos' present price is competitive with other red Bordeaux, the Prats demonstrated that growers can produce and market great wine without degenerating into grasping money hounds.

The estate of Haut-Brion reminds me of an urban park. One of the oldest vineyards in Bordeaux, the property has come to be surrounded by apartment buildings. Until 1955 it was considered the best of the first growths, but aggressive marketing (and winemaking) by other châteaux somewhat eclipsed Haut-Brion's reputation. At least since the Second World War Haut-Brion has been producing the sort of wines which puzzle tastebuds accustomed to "classical Bordeaux"—the wines seem ready dazzlingly early. In his book on Bordeaux, David Peppercorn comments on a 1979 tasting to assess the progress of the 1975s. He found the wine was "extremely attractive but, in startling contrast to the other first growths, seemed already drinkable." Recent vintages, the 1981, 1982 and 1983 wines, have received spectacular reviews and the vineyard seems to be regaining some of its earlier glory. The estate also makes a very small amount of white which, due to its rarity (1,500 cases) and its reputation for longevity, makes an ideal investment wine.

The Gaja family, aside from being the most well-known name in Barbaresco, also has the distinction of representing Romanée-Conti in Italy. Angelo Gaja is a marketing leader in the style of Robert Mondavi. Both men recognize that the ability to distribute their wines counts almost as much as the wines' quality. Fine Italian wines have often languished in obscurity for lack of a talented distributor. The fact that Gaja offers Barbaresco futures also shows the progressive inclination of his firm.

Château Cantemerle is a fifth-growth that could easily attain Ducru/Las-Cases status in the next couple of years. The French firm of Cordier bought the estate in 1981; they acquired a great vineyard, then updated it with modern equipment. A charming rationale, probably apocryphal, states that the Cantemerle only ranked as a fifth-growth in the classification of 1855 because the wagon carrying the samples to the Paris exhibition broke a wheel en route. The wine arrived late and the château's name was appended to the roster of fifth-growths as something of an afterthought, a tale that gains credence when you see Cantemerle's name scrawled in tiny writing at the very bottom of the list of classified wines. In my opinion the wine has tasted consistently better than its official rank; the 1983 Cantemerle was considered the best of the vintage in its class. At this point I'd practically buy Cantemerle blindfolded—in any vintage.

I selected Château d'Yquem for its uniqueness and its IGW value. In general 1980 was a poor year (excessively light wines) for most of Bordeaux, but an outstanding year for d'Yquem. This Sauternes produces its best wines in light years, because of the natural concentration of sugar in the grapes. The result is amazingly long-lived sweet wine. The 1980 is often compared favorably with the 1970 (described as lasting until 2070).

I have to admit to having a financial interest in Rutherford Ranch, prompted by my impression of its quality. For a while the vineyard awarded me exclusive rights to distribute their Napa Cabernet in New York, although by the time this book is published my exclusivity will have ended. The wine knocked me over when I first tasted it in California, recalling the depth of a Latour with woody overtones. The wine has the concentration of fruit and tannin only found in wines designed to last.

I listed three commercial shippers for Corton-Charlemagne because only about 600 cases make it to this country. All are expensive, although not in the league of other extravagantly priced white Burgundies like the Le Montrachet of Domaine de la Romanée-Conti. Corton-Charle-magne has a long history as an investment wine, with cases appearing regularly in the international auction market. Connoisseurs of white Burgundy immediately recognize its name and its style which, like reds structured to last a long time, may require several years before revealing itself.

Richebourg, along with La Tâche in the previous portfolio, is an-other of the vineyards belonging to the Domaine de la Romanée-Conti. Wine from the Romanée-Conti vineyard itself is almost never avail-able, despite the fact that ostensibly fifty percent of its tiny production is shipped to the U.S. Altogether there are six wines produced from a total area of just over fifty acres. The ones to buy for investment are Romanée-Conti (if you ever see a case of it that costs less than a new sports sedan), La Tâche and Richebourg, all of which are reds; and Le Montrachet, the Domaine's white. All the wines have histories of high resale prices and reputations for longevity atypical for Burgundy.

Michael Broadbent, head of Christie's wine department, recently informed me that 1975 is a sleeper year for Port, that the value of the vintage has not yet been recognized; in consequence, prices are still low. Considering the recent behavior of the Port market, it's only a matter of time before bargain hunters sniff out this one and its price begins to hop upward like its fellows.

CHAPTER SEVEN

PROTECTING YOUR INVESTMENT

STORAGE

Wine lovers can extoll the virtues of a vineyard's soil, they can tally up the days of sunshine or rain and they can judge an oenologists's skill by the number of great wines he's coaxed from his roster of vineyards, but once a wine is in the bottle one factor becomes preeminent in determining the wine's future—storage. Hiccups in the market, the influence of fad and fashion, bad weather and poor vintages, each presents a danger to the investment value of wine. But bad storage kills investment-grade wine.

I once had a conversation in a sauna with the eminent food and restaurant expert, Saul Zabar. While the two of us sweated away our sins we swapped wine and food stories. At one point he mopped his brow and confessed to having done a horrible thing to his wine.

Oh? And what would that have been?

He explained that he had a collection of very special red Bordeaux, famous vintages from the forties and fifties, which he kept in his summer home. He shook his head and looked away. The problem was, he knew that the basement of his summer house was just too damn hot to store wine, but what with one thing and another he had never gotten around to moving them. Now he was afraid to open them, fearing they'd turned.

A few weeks later we met to taste the wines. He had reasoned correctly. I don't think I've ever had a tasting experience as depressing as that afternoon's. Sampling his precious bottles was like strolling through a magnificent ruin: the labels were all that remained to indicate the former glory of each vineyard. His 1949 Cheval Blanc, purchased for $2.99 and now worth $125 a bottle, was vinegar. His 1945 Mouton-Rothschild was gone; the same with his 1947 Pétrus. The wine had roasted to death. Keep wines cool.

The lesson was plain: if you can't store wine, don't buy it.

ELEMENTS OF PROPER STORAGE

These are the elements for ideal storage:

- □ A temperature of fifty-five degrees Fahrenheit
- □ No bright light or fluorescent lighting
- □ Protection against vibration and odor
- □ Sixty percent humidity

This describes the *ideal* cellar. In an imperfect world however, we have to be prepared to compromise. Fifty-five degrees is the temperature most often found in a Burgundy *cave*, a Bordeaux *chais* or, for that matter, the cellar of an English manor. Long experience has shown us that wine ages slowest in a cool environment. Several double magnums of 1865 Lafite which I've owned have come from Scottish castles, where the wine slept undisturbed in an underground crypt for over a hundred years. Still, long-lived wines are somewhat flexible when it comes to temperature, especially in their youth. Sudden changes in temperature are the most harmful to wine. A home cellar that shifts between fifty and seventy degrees over the course of a season, while not ideal, is acceptable. A twenty-degree change in a single day, however, might seriously damage the wine. Sustained high temperatures will age a wine without allowing its elements to harmonize. One summer in a hot base-ment will not turn a raw, leathery first-growth into a round, mature wine; rather, you'll end up with an astringent stringy wine (if not vin-egar) with all the flesh stripped from its bones.

Older wines are less forgiving of any temperature variation. If you plan on purchasing wines older than fifteen years, either take the steps necessary to keep them in a consistently cool environment at home or store them professionally.

Winemakers have long known that light affects wine, hence the use of dark-colored bottles. Wine is particularly vulnerable to fluores-cent lighting. In the early seventies I was approached by a Rensselaer scientist to sponsor an actinic lamp he had invented for artificially ag-ing wine; I even held a demonstration for the press in my shop. A frame held two plates of transparent glass about a centimeter apart. Wine was poured between the layers of glass, forming a thin sheet of liquid which was then exposed to the light for thirty or forty seconds. A striking change in color resulted from the exposure; the bright red of a young wine deepened into the orange-brick timbre of a mature vin-tage. The transition was not as successful where taste was concerned. Different wines reacted with varying results. Highly acidic wines bene-fited the most, softening and losing some of their edge after treatment. An inexpensive brandy showed radical improvement after a moment's exposure, taking on the smooth roundness of a more expensive aged spirit. The actinic lamp, to my knowledge, never went anywhere. Occasionally I dream of the fabulous vintages we could drink for everyday wines if we could mature bottles in minutes instead of years, and then I sense how much romance and mystery we would also lose. I'm glad the light didn't catch on.

Vibration represents another peril to fine wine. Vibration is less a problem with storage (unless you live over a subway) than transportation. Roger Livdahl, one of the premier wine appraisers in the United States, discounts wine which hasn't been bottled at the château or winery. Part of the discount relates to the shade of doubt regarding authenticity which is always present when a wine is not estate-bottled. But the greater rationale pertains to the additional rough handling the wine may have received in passing through so many hands (estate-*négociant*-shipper-importer-bottler) before bottling, treatment which may shorten the life span of the wine. Move your wines from place to place or cellar to cellar as little as possible. If, perchance, you find yourself investing in wines in the English market (not inconceivable if the pound were to substantially weaken), try to store your purchases in England. Facilities are inexpensive and often easily arranged through an auction house or broker. Your wine will be more valuable in the long run if it isn't shuttled back and forth across the Atlantic.

Excessive humidity encourages the growth of fungus; and fungus eats at the label and cork. Allowed to continue unchecked, the fungal aroma of the cork will penetrate the wine, giving it an "off" flavor (hence, "corked" wine). The resale value of wine is also partially a function of the bottle condition; if the labels are falling off (indicating excessively dry storage) or rotting away (too much humidity), the wine will be worth less than the same bottles whose labels are impeccable.

High humidity also makes it easier for ambient odors to affect the wine. I once tainted a valued case of Romanée-Conti by leaving it in a closet during the summertime. My apartment was air-conditioned, so I wasn't concerned about the temperature, but my wife stored some winter coats lined with mothballs in the same closet. The wine carried an unmistakable aroma of mothballs for several months after I moved it out of the closet into a storage vault. The taint faded as the wine rested in a cellar with proper ventilation, but for almost a year I waited on needles and pins to see if I had inadvertently destroyed my wine.

WHERE DO I STORE MY WINE?

Finding good storage is sometimes the most difficult aspect of wine investment. Having your own on-premises cellar permits you to exercise your "dual liquidity" option at any time—that is, after picking out a bottle, you may either sell it or drink it. When a new client purchases an expensive wine from me and asks if he can store it in his air-conditioned basement I have to answer with a qualified yes. Having learned from experience about the threat an active family sometimes poses to expensive bottles, I don't store much wine at home. A small climate-controlled wine vault, about the size of the refrigerator, serves as the resting place for wines en route to the Sokolin dinner table. A much larger vault at my Madison Avenue shop houses individual bottles of rare wines. Our fine wines rest in air-conditioned comfort in a commercial warehouse; we transport them to the shop as needed or deliver them directly to a client's home or storage facility.

I'm ashamed to admit that the finest storage facilities I've ever seen belong to devoted collectors, rather than members of the wine trade. One wine lover of my acquaintance bought an abandoned speakeasy located beneath Dag Hammarskjold Plaza in New York City; columns arch into groined vaults overhead and on one wall a mosaic dating from the days of Prohibition depicts cavorting revelers. A southern physician with an insatiable appetite for wine converted a hillside behind his house into a facility that would make many a wholesaler envious—as well it should, for the doctor has almost $10 million invested in vintage wines. Another client who loves oversize bottles has a wine cellar several stories above Fifth Avenue, his treasures lovingly enclosed in custom-made glass-fronted cases with climate control, alarm system and a backup power source wired into each case. Strolling through the carpeted aisles of his cellar is like stepping into a science fiction film; the double magnums and imperials resemble astronauts in suspended animation during a very long journey into the future, which, in a sense, they are.

Storing wine at home need not be such an extravagant venture to be effective, as long as you pay attention to the basic requirements. If you're doubtful about temperature or humidity, take a few readings in your intended storage space over the course of several days. An inexpensive thermometer and humidistat will do the trick nicely.

Insulated, climate-controlled wine vaults may be purchased in various sizes, at fairly modest prices. Your wine merchant can recommend a manufacturer or dealer, or you can investigate the various cellar makers yourself. Most of them advertise in wine magazines or in newspapers. A climate-controlled closet or cupboard will also suffice. If you have limited resources, reserve your wine vault for your wines with investment value. I have one client who used to peruse the "For Sale" sections of restaurant trade publications until he found exactly what he wanted at a liquidation sale: a used walk-in refrigerator. He put the thing in his garage and now has a superior cellar.

Always store your bottles on their sides, so that the wine touches the corks, keeping them moist. Dry corks can shrink, allowing air to enter the bottles. If you don't store your wine in its original case, use wooden or metal beehive racks, insuring minimal disturbance when removing any single bottle. Tags with the name of each wine will also diminish the need to examine (and move) each bottle.

PROFESSIONAL STORAGE

A few years of purchasing IGW can add up to a substantial storage problem, in which case the best alternative may be to look for professional space. As wines get older they become more fragile, more vulnerable to cellar conditions that deviate from the ideal. Unless you've taken steps to create an ideal storage environment in your home, you may want to consider professional storage, at least for your IGWs.

Not all professional storage is created equal. Some warehouses cater to wine—most do not. As a rule, you pay more for space which guarantees ideal cellar conditions. Washington, Chicago, New York and Los Angeles all have facilities for private collectors wishing to store wine. A very few wine merchants also offer storage, after sale, for their clients. California seems to be the leader in the field, with many retailers offering their clients locker space to store their fine wines. If your area doesn't have either of these amenities, then look for cool warehouse space, with temperature, humidity and lighting conditions as outlined above. Be creative; a friend of mine located a furrier who rents him space in his cold storage warehouse.

If you do find a wine-oriented facility, here are some considerations in addition to the basic guidelines:

  □ Cellar liability
  □ Backup systems in case of power failure
  □ Security
  □ A willingness to issue an affidavit of storage

The extra cost of storing your wine in a professional facility should be offset by the premium paid for perfectly stored IGW. A certificate or affidavit from the facility is your proof of proper storage; it should list your wines and the period of storage. If a warehouse offering space specifically for wine use is unwilling to provide this sort of certification, look elsewhere for storage. It's not worth the extra cost for cellar conditions if you can't prove you stored your wine properly.

Recently, I was asked to evaluate five cases of IGW from 1961. The owner was proud of his holdings; they had been in his home cellar for twenty years. His prospective buyer wanted an appraisal before the sale. I studied his 1961 Cheval Blanc (original purchase price in 1964: $70 per case). The wine looked a little cloudy to me; we opened one bottle and found it had turned to vinegar. Apparently, his cellar had been hot at various times, and there had been some fluorescent lighting nearby. Bottles which should have been worth $300 were ruined. His original investment of a few thousand dollars should have been worth $150,000. Instead, his cellar was worth about $400, the display value of the bottles, if indeed he could find a buyer.

RECORKING AND REFILLING

IGW older than forty years should be recorked as a matter of course; whether you want to go to the additional expense of having the bottles topped off with more wine is a personal decision. Roger Livdahl takes close account of ullage (the amount of wine lost through slow evaporation) in his appraisals; you'll also notice that auction catalogues meticulously describe the fill level of rare bottles ("low neck/high shoulder fill"; "low shoulder fill"). Under ideal storage conditions, the fill level of wine drops at the rate of one centimeter every ten years, according to Livdahl. A wine with an inappropriately low fill is discounted accordingly.

Recorking and refilling can only be done at the original château or vineyard. An exception to this is Château Lafite which annually sends a team to the United States to service older bottles for American collectors. A bottle which has been recorked and topped off has a higher value than a wine of the same date which has not.

In 1960, I purchased a case of 1928 Haut-Brion for $33. In 1968, I opened a bottle and it tasted extraordinary. However, it still tasted young and in my opinion would benefit by further aging. The cork was softening and I had the wine recorked in New York (I didn't know any better). In 1984, I again tasted a bottle; it was outstanding, definitely ready to drink. However, by now the 1968 corks were loose.

I sent the wine to Château Haut-Brion. They used one bottle to top off the remainder of the case, then inserted new corks. The wine is now sold for $5,000 per case, so I am the beneficiary of a delightful increase.

INSURANCE

Taking the trouble to store fine wine properly and then not insuring it is like buying an expensive horse and then not locking the barn door. The standard homeowner's policy makes no special provisions for wine. In the event of disaster, your coverage may not even indemnify you for the original purchase price on particularly expensive bottles. This situation is remedied in two ways: you can either request a rider to your homeowner's policy that will extend your coverage to include your bottles of fine wine; or you can purchase a policy designed exclusively for the protection of wine cellars.

Jules Epstein is the President of Joseph G. Gray & Co. Insurance; he is also a wine lover. After dropping a bottle from his own collection, a 1966 La Mission-Haut-Brion, he realized that his own homeowner's policy wouldn't cover the loss. Necessity is the mother of invention. He created a policy tailored specifically for wine cellars, now underwritten by the National Union Fire Insurance Company. A sample application follows on pages 84 and 85.

Whether you wish to insure your wine with its own policy or as an add-on to your homeowner's coverage, you should look for protection against fire, theft, flood, excessive vibration and accidental breakage. If climate-control equipment is used in the storage facility your coverage should also protect you against any loss as a result of equipment or power failure.

If you store your wine in a professional facility you will almost certainly need an individual policy. (Epstein's policy covers both commercial and private space.) Facilities should gladly explain the limits of their own liability before renting you space.

Your policy will most likely not cover you for the following contingencies:

- An act of war
- Mysterious disappearance
- Ullage
- Temperature changes (except in climate-controlled settings)
- Radiation
- Mold or rot
- Insects, vermin or rodents
- Spoilage

This type of coverage is just about the same as that sought by wine merchants. The factor to keep uppermost in your mind is the extent of liability. A typical insurance company will want to have the following information about your collection: the number of bottles you keep, their size, a description which includes château and type (that is, Bordeaux, Port, Sauterne, Burgundy, etc.), the vintage, and the current market value of each. This may mean having an appraisal of your collection done by a creditable appraiser or wine merchant, or reaching some other type of agreement with the insurers about what they will accept as "fair market value." Prices fetched at public auctions are sometimes accepted as fair market value, or prices listed by certain wine merchants might be acceptable.

Insurers will also want to know if your cellar or storage area is

NATIONAL UNION
FIRE INSURANCE COMPANY
OF PITTSBURGH, PA.

EXECUTIVE OFFICES: 70 Pine Street, New York, NY 10270

A Capital Stock Company

APPLICATION FOR FINE WINE INSURANCE   Not Available in Texas

(Please complete carefully. This application forms part of your policy.)

I. APPLICANT INFORMATION

Applicant's Name: _____

Mailing Address: _____

_____

Occupation: _____

II. LOCATION(S) OF STORAGE. Complete the applicable section(s) for all locations where insured wines will be stored.

Primary Residence

Address: _____

Owned or leased dwelling? _____

Single attached, single unattached, or multi-unit structure? _____

What is the construction of the residence? _____

Is the residence equipped with a burglar alarm or security system? No____ Yes____ If yes, please describe. _____

Is the residence equipped with a fire detection or alarm system? No____ Yes____ If yes, please describe. _____

Please describe the location and construction of the wine storage area. _____

Is the wine storage area climate controlled? No____ Yes____ If yes, please describe the type of climate control equipment used. _____

What is the total value of wines stored at this location, as per the attached inventory schedule? $_____

Secondary Residence (Copy and complete this section as needed for additional residences and attach to the application.)

Address: _____

Owned or leased dwelling? _____

Single attached, single unattached, or multi-unit structure? _____

What is the construction of the residence? _____

Is the residence equipped with a burglar alarm or security system? No____ Yes____ If yes, please describe. _____

Is the residence equipped with a fire detection or alarm system? No____ Yes____ If yes, please describe. _____

Please describe the location and construction of the wine storage area. _____

Is the wine storage area climate controlled? No____ Yes____ If yes, please describe the type of climate control equipment used. _____

What is the total value of wines stored at this location, as per the attached inventory schedule? $_____

Public Warehouse (Copy and complete this section as needed for additional warehouses and attach to the application.)

Name of Warehouse: _____

Address: _____

Name of Warehouse Representative: _____ Telephone Number: (____) _____

How long have your wines been stored at this warehouse? _____

What is the total value of wines stored at this location, as per the attached inventory schedule? $_____

FW
42103 (4/85)

AIG **A Member Company of American International Group**

I. LOSS HISTORY

Have you had any wine losses during the past three years? No _____ Yes _____ If yes, please explain. _____

_____

Have you had any property losses during the past three years? No _____ Yes _____ If yes, please explain. _____

_____

V. INVENTORY SCHEDULE(S)   (NOTE: The attached inventory schedule form must be completed in full for each location of storage listed in Section II, LOCATION(S) OF STORAGE.)

Are the values listed on the attached inventory schedule(s) your own estimates or those of an appraiser? _____

List date of appraisal and name of appraiser, if applicable: Date of Appraisal: _____

Name of Appraiser: _____ Telephone Number: ( )

Mailing Address: _____

V. SELF RATING - Only complete this section if the total value of all wines to be insured (the sum of the limit(s) of liability specified on the inventory schedule(s) is $50,000 or less.

Will insured wines be stored at more than three locations or in more than one public warehouse?   Yes _____ No _____

Are any required inventory schedule forms not completed in full or not attached to this application?   Yes _____ No _____

Are any wines to be insured valued at, or in excess of, $500 per bottle or $3,600 per case?   Yes _____ No _____

Have you had any wine losses in the last three years?   Yes _____ No _____

If you answered YES to ANY of the above questions, you are not eligible for self rating and a premium quotation will be extended to you upon receipt of your application.

If you answered NO to ALL of the above questions, the annual rate for your policy is $5 per $1,000 of insurance. Complete the following steps in order to have your policy in force immediately after approval of your application.
1) Compute the annual premium based on this rate and the value of all wines to be insured.
   (NOTE: A minimum premium of $50 is charged if the value of all wines to be insured is $10,000 or less.)
2) List your annual premium payment: $ _____
3) Attach your check for the full amount of the annual premium.

_____

This application does not bind the applicant or the Company, but it is agreed that this form shall be the basis of the contract should a policy be issued, and it will be attached to and made a part of the policy. The applicant represents that if the information supplied on this application changes between the date of this application and the time when the policy is issued, the applicant will immediately notify the Company of such changes.

I declare the answers in this application are, to the best of my knowledge and belief, true and complete and I agree that:
1. The insurance on scheduled wines shall become effective after all of the following conditions have been met:
   a. The full amount of the annual premium has been paid; and
   b. The Company has approved the application according to its established limits, rules and standards.
2. The Company is not bound by any statements made by or to any agent unless such statements are written in this application and accepted by the Company.
3. Acceptance of the policy, containing a copy of the application, by me is acknowledgement and ratification of any modifications made in the application, and that no change in the current values and limit of liability specified on the inventory schedule(s) and the total limit of liability in the aggregate over all locations will be made unless agreed to in writing by the Company.

NOTICE TO NEW YORK APPLICANTS: ANY PERSON WHO KNOWINGLY AND WITH INTENT TO DEFRAUD ANY INSURANCE COMPANY OR OTHER PERSON FILES AN APPLICATION FOR INSURANCE CONTAINING ANY FALSE INFORMATION, OR CONCEALS FOR THE PURPOSE OF MISLEADING, INFORMATION CONCERNING ANY FACT MATERIAL THERETO, COMMITS A FRAUDULENT INSURANCE ACT, WHICH IS A CRIME.

_____   _____
Signature of Applicant   Date

equipped with security and smoke alarms or fire detection systems, the location and construction of the area, whether the area is climate controlled, type of climate-control equipment used and type of backup for this system.

This information, including the estimated fair market value of the wine, should be updated at least every two years, and in the case of rapidly appreciating wine, every year. In the event of a loss, the insurance company will generally have the option of either reimbursing you or replacing your wine.

In 1986, a typical premium was $5 for each $1,000 of insured property, for all wine valued at less than $500 per bottle or less than $3,600 per case. Above those values, premiums need to be individually factored. Clearly if you store costly wine haphazardly your insurance rates will be exorbitant.

In the chapter on strategy I recommend that you keep a cellar book or record. It comes in handy when purchasing insurance. Cellar records should include these entries: the name and year of the wine in each bottle, the total amount of each type purchased, from whom, on what date, the name of the shipper and the price paid. If you drink the wine rather than sell it (or drink one bottle), you should also enter your own comments on taste and the date, adjacent to the other technical information.

APPRAISALS

How do you assess the value of your wine? By having it appraised. The two primary reasons for an appraisal are insurance and sale. Roger Livdahl asserts that the single most accurate assessment by a private collector of the worth of his own cellar was off by *seventeen percent*! Most amateur estimates are wildly awry. Private collectors just don't have the time, expertise, and information to make accurate appraisals. You would be wise to have your wine appraised every two years or so, just in the interest of keeping yourself informed.

Wine merchants sometimes do appraisals, or can recommend a creditable appraiser. Don't hesitate to ask for the credentials of whomever you're considering for the job. At the very minimum, the appraiser should have a working knowledge of the current retail and auction prices and some sense of market trends. The work of Roger Livdahl, a California appraiser, is a model for the field, and represents the quality and detail you should demand from an appraiser.

Livdahl was a collector himself for twenty years and he needed to keep informed about the value of his wines for insurance purposes. He realized that other collectors, as well as those administering estates, often needed similar information on the value of rare wine. Many merchants simply do not have the time to maintain up-to-the-minute files on the thousands of vintages and names about which collectors inquire. Livdahl filled a void in the industry, and began working as a wine consultant and evaluator.

Livdahl maintains information on the value of over 20,000 wines ranging over 275 years. Harriet Lembeck, a New York appraiser who also teaches and writes about wine, has also compiled a data base of prices. Both Livdahl and Lembeck feel that the more information available about a wine the greater the accuracy of the appraisal. Both appraisers update their information monthly with reports from auction and retail sales in Europe and the U.S.

Lembeck offers a word of advice for those considering an appraiser: "Beware anyone who bases their fee on a percentage of the cellar's appraised value. There's always the temptation to inflate the wine's worth."

SECURITY

Last year a client spent $120,000 in my shop in the course of an afternoon. He didn't take delivery until the weekend, insisting that I personally drive the truck to his Long Island home under the cover of darkness. I thought my truck-unloading days were long behind me, but when I arrived it was just the two us; we spent the better part of three hours hustling the wine into his house.

The man has a cellar that extends five stories underground; a heliport in his backyard allows him to commute by air to Manhattan each day. He is, to put it mildly, concerned about security.

Wine theft is a serious and often unreported problem. Unless the victim is directly involved in the wine trade—a merchant, a wholesaler or restaurant—he rarely notifies the press. The last thing a wealthy collector wants to do is draw attention to his rare bottles. The wealthy or well-known personalities who have been robbed almost always try to avoid any publicity surrounding the theft. In the early 1980s, one New York retailer lost $60,000 worth of wine when his home cellar was looted; a California entertainer was robbed of $120,000 worth of wine from his home; and a Long Island attorney had 830 select bottles, worth $372,000, removed from his private cellar while other nearby bottles were untouched. In each of these cases, the thieves knew precisely what to take and what they did not want; they were wine experts themselves. (Life does sometimes provide amusing alternatives; when a London restaurant was robbed of its wines last year, the thieves concentrated exclusively on inexpensive red Bordeaux wines, pushing aside the far more valuable collection of rare California Cabernets.) The lack of reporting of wine crime makes it difficult for authorities to track down the criminals or the wine.

To address the issue of wine theft, Livdahl has created the National Rare Wine Registry (NRWR). The NRWR identifies and registers wines by both a visible marking on the label, and an invisible code marked on the bottle itself. The mark is changed at the time of resale, at no charge to the new owner. Livdahl's mark on the labels alerts a thief, collector or retailer that the wine is part of a registered collection. The invisible code identifies the owner, making it easy to return the wine in the event of its recovery. The wine trade has hailed the system as an effective method of discouraging theft. In my opinion, the NRWR lends an extra element of integrity to collections, particularly those with rare bottles. For further information, contact the National Rare Wine Registry, 2157 North Vine Street #8, Los Angeles, CA 90068; (213) 460-7029.

OCCASIONAL TASTING

One final note on protection of your investment: taste your IGW once in a while. The portfolios in Chapter Six include bottles for tasting. Don't become so obsessed with the appreciation of your wine that you deny yourself the pleasure of marking its progress toward maturity. In the last five years some wines have appreciated so quickly that many of my clients can't bring themselves to open a bottle. "It's too expensive for me to drink!" they cry. Nonsense. Taste it now and then or you'll never know why people are willing to pay so much money for wine.

CHAPTER EIGHT

SELLING YOUR WINE

If most state governments had their druthers, the only way you could sell your wine would be to die, go bankrupt or get a divorce. Short of these extreme circumstances, states take a dim view of private individuals hawking their old bottles. Two oases offer an alternative to this narrow-minded outlook. California collectors may sell their wine back to retailers, as long as the red wine is at least ten years old and the white wine is at least five. Wine lovers in Illinois have it slightly easier; they can sell back to wholesalers without regard for the age of the wine.

Unlike Europe, the U.S. has no states where you're allowed to walk over to your neighbor's, knock on his door and offer him a great deal on the extra case of Richebourg you've been hiding under your stairs.

Which is not to say that it isn't done. The "quiet market" is an active network of collectors who buy, sell and swap wines illegally. It's an open secret in the wine trade that several prominent consultants keep bread on the table and wine in the glass by facilitating such arrangements. Members of the wine trade disagree sharply about the size and scope of such transactions. One wine consultant with whom I talked dismissed the whole idea of an underground market. "Boil it down and you've got a bunch of collectors swapping bottles during a weekend in Atlantic City. It's peanuts by comparison to the legal volume."

State officials are generally loathe to acknowledge that illegal trades occur with any frequency; their investigators are already swamped with violations at the retail and wholesale level. Who wants to finance a drive to stamp out the illegal wine market?

Before you let such attitudes lull you into thinking about selling your wine illegally, consider the remote, but real, chance of getting caught. Craig Goldwyn, in an article for the *Wine Review*, cites the instance of a New Jersey collector who advertised the sale of his cellar. Investigators for the New Jersey Alcohol and Beverage Commission noticed the ad, arrested him and confiscated his cellar, later liquidating it at public auction. The collector was out $30,000 in wine. It would seem that those who succeed in the quiet market do it discreetly.

A quick run-through of the advertisements of many wine newsletters indicates that despite the chance of getting caught, many wine lovers do indeed sell their wine directly to private buyers. Collectors tell me they resent the state telling them what they can and cannot do with their wines. Private sales between individuals are quite common in Europe and those nations do not seem to have suffered from them.

American wine lovers should realize that the law denies them the protection their European counterparts presently enjoy. If you're dissatisfied with a wine you purchase in the wine underground, to whom will you complain? What state agency will pursue your cause? What lawyer will undertake your suit? If you get burned, you stay burned. And aside from whatever damage you might inflict on your enemy by bad-mouthing him among other potential buyers, you can exact no retribution. If you're going to buy from an unlicensed individual, then make sure the wine has been appraised by someone you trust—it's the only guarantee you have you're not buying a pig in a poke.

SELLING LEGALLY—THE AUCTION MARKET

The largest legal outlet for your wines, the American auction market, sold between $6 million and $7 million worth of wine in 1986. American wine auctions have been around for less than a decade, and are still in their infancy. The Chicago Wine Company (CWC), the largest auctioneer of wine in America, put its first case of wine on the block in 1978. Since then, Christie's, in Chicago, and Butterfield and Butterfield, in San Francisco, both firms with extensive auctioneering experience, have begun competing for rare and fine wines from American cellars. U.S. auctions have a long way to go before they catch up to their European counterparts; still, it's a beginning.

Depending on whom you talk to, exactly what constitutes an auction tends to waffle, so it's best if we draw a few distinctions. In the most common sense of the word, an auction is a public event, a gathering where buyers publicly bid on goods arranged in specified lots. Typically the bidding progresses in prearranged increments ($20, say) and a lot, as it pertains to wine, may range in quantity from a single bottle on up to hundreds of cases. In this country at least, lots generally involve no more than a case or two of wine at a time, although multiple lots of the same wine may offer different buyers chances at the same goods. Also, auctioneers, by history and tradition, sell goods on consignment; that is, while an auction house may take possession of somebody's wine, it doesn't actually own it. The original seller owns the wine until the bang of auctioneer's gavel indicates a sale has been made, at which point ownership transfers to the successful bidder. The auction house serves as the seller's representative in the transaction; it never actually *owns* the wine.

In the American auction arena there's a sort of gentlemanly disagreement about which firms run "real" auctions, and which firms just pretend to. Christie's, Butterfield and Butterfield and the Chicago Wine Company, for example, never actually own any of the wine sold at their auctions. But the Texas Art Gallery (TAG), which sponsors a fine and rare wine auction in Dallas every year, owns *all* the wine it sells. The Texas Art Gallery finds its wine in the way that retailers in other states do—it buys it from wholesalers. The gallery also has a retail wine business. Traditional firms say this arrangement violates the spirit of an auction—which is to see what an open process of bidding will bring, high *or* low. By acting like retailers, such auctioneers already have a built-in reserve (a price below which the wine will not be sold); critics also say arrangements like the Texas Art Gallery's muddy the distinction between retailers, who concentrate on recent vintages of wine, and auction houses, whose stock-in-trade are older wines.

The Texas Art Gallery defends itself by saying that state law forbids it from accepting wines on consignment from private individuals (the established practice of auctioneers in California and Illinois). TAG also points out that it regularly sells wines at auction for less than the price of the same wines offered in its retail operation. "Auction fever," it points out, accounts for wines that sometimes sell for a higher price at auction than in its retail store.

I can sympathize with the Texans. I've held two auctions in New York, with the express purpose of testing the popularity of the concept of reselling wine. New York authorities wouldn't permit me to sell other people's wines, so I sold my own. At both auctions bidders paid less for their wines than my retail customers.

Auctioneers also take sides over whether an auction ought to be public and whether a firm ought to have all of the lots offered in its physical possession at the site of the auction. In England it's quite common to see a phrase appended to a lot's description listing the geographic location of the cellar where the wine is presently stored ("lying in Norfolk" or "lying in Essex"). With old and valued customers English firms have established bonds of trust.

In America, where proper storage cannot be so easily taken for granted, it's customary for wine to be in the possession of the auctioneer, and sometimes even available for inspection and tasting by interested buyers. Not all firms adhere to this policy. If you have doubts, inquire about the specific lot that interests you. Simply because a wine isn't available for inspection shouldn't automatically disqualify it from your consideration, but you should be aware that the more remote you are from any given wine, the less likely you are to detect any flaws before buying it.

Chicago Wine Company, perhaps less harnessed to the shackles of tradition because the auction business is only one part of the company (it also has extensive retail and wholesale operations), holds "silent" auctions as well as public ones, another practice that riles purists. Participants receive a catalogue listing the wines, as in a regular auction, then they're invited to mail their bids to the firm. The highest bid takes the lot.

As a seller, whether you want to offer your wine at a silent or public auction may be a matter of individual preference and scheduling. How important is it for you to actually see your wine "knocked down" (auction-speak for sold)? How much do you trust the auction house? All auctioneers agree that there's a certain psychological satisfaction in seeing your astute purchases of a decade past inspire a pitched bidding battle. On the other hand, if the next conveniently scheduled auction is silent, or you weren't considering making the trip to Chicago or San Francisco anyway, then perhaps the fact that an auction is silent isn't a major concern.

In looking for an auction to sell your wine, you ought to consider several issues: the house percentage of knockdowns (the percentage of wines listed in a catalogue which are actually sold); whether it charges buyer/seller premiums and if so, how much; the house's willingness to quote previous sale prices for wines similar or identical to your own; and finally, the age of the wine you wish to sell.

All three of the firms whose auctions accept wine from private collectors claim knockdown percentages of over ninety percent. John Hart, executive vice president of the Chicago Wine Company, said that the percentage was "slightly lower" (while not naming an exact figure) for CWC's silent auctions, a condition he attributed to the unusually large numbers of lots typically offered in a silent auction. Christie's and Butterfield and Butterfield publish lists of sale prices after each auction, available if you write to either firm. CWC does not publish lists, but John Hart is amenable to quoting prices from both public and silent auctions over the telephone.

Premiums are percentages of the sale price, paid by the buyer, the seller, or both. Whether a firm charges a premium and, if so, how such premiums are established varies quite a bit from firm to firm, so it's a good idea to ask about it before committing yourself. Some firms charge a fixed percentage of the sale price as a premium; others fix the premium according to the individual wine.

The age of the wines you wish to sell will also have some bearing on where you decide to sell. The California restriction regarding young wines applies to auction sales in addition to private sales to retailers. Practically speaking, this means Butterfield and Butterfield is unlikely to handle the sale of your 1982 red wines until 1992 (unless you happen to die, in which case it will cheerfully liquidate your wines, recent vintages included). None of the major firms (Butterfield and Butterfield included) want to be perceived as competing with the retail wine market. Aside from considerations of volume (the younger a vintage the more of it there is around), auction houses concentrate on older vintages because they're rarer and more valuable.

The procedure for selling your wines at auction is fairly simple. The first thing to do is mail the list of wines you wish to sell to your auction house of choice; names and addresses of firms and their officials are listed below. A representative of the firm will notify you of its interest. In instances of large cellars or rare wines, someone from the auction may want to inspect your offerings in person. You will then discuss the specifics of the company's procedures and the likely return you may expect on your wines. (Having had your cellar recently appraised can be of great help at this point.) Assuming that you reach an agreement, the next step will be to ship your wines to the auction site, where they will be inspected. If all is as it should be, your wines will appear in the next auction catalogue, with a suggested range of opening bids.

All of the houses offered good advice for this book. Michael Davis cautions people to take the trouble to learn their local laws; some basic familiarity with the legal requirements for shipping wine out of your home state (generally pretty easy) or importing it into your home state (moderately to extremely difficult) can avert future hassles. John Hart counsels would-be sellers to pay special attention to storage. CWC rejects wine more often for poor storage than for any other single reason. Dennis Foley, of Butterfield and Butterfield, suggests that sellers keep in mind that auction sales balance themselves out; that unexpectedly high or low returns usually work out to a pretty good average.

What follows is a list of the major auction houses. No two of them are exactly alike. The Chicago Wine Company, for example, does an extensive retail and wholesale business (with one of the largest Bordeaux inventories in the world) in addition to its auctions. Christie's and Butterfield and Butterfield are auctioneers in the traditional manner, with no stocks of their own. The latter firms sell American cellars exclusively in the U.S. (Christie's has a firm policy of not shipping wines back to Europe for resale, for fear that too much traveling will damage fine wine.) CWC, on the other hand, will sometimes counsel an American to consider selling his wines at one of their London auctions.

The Chicago Wine Company
5663 Howard Street
Niles, IL 60648
(312) 647-8789
contact: John H. Hart

Two or three public auctions annually in Chicago; five public auctions annually in London; five silent auctions annually, handled through Chicago.

Christie's (Chicago)   *Five public auctions annually, all in Chi-*
200 West Superior   *cago.*
Chicago, IL 60610
(312) 951-1011
contact: Michael Davis

Christie's (London)   *For specifics of European schedule, write*
8 King Street   *to London office.*
Saint James's
London SW1Y 6QT England
(441) 839-9060
contact: Michael Broadbent

Butterfield and Butterfield   *Six public auctions annually, all in San*
220 San Bruno Avenue   *Francisco.*
San Francisco, CA 94103
(415) 861-7500
contact: Dennis Foley

Sotheby Parke Bernet   *Sotheby's does not hold wine auctions in*
1334 York Avenue   *America, nor do they have a resident*
New York, NY 10021   *wine expert in the U.S.; however, their*
(212) 606-7000   *London office provides information on*
                                  their European wine auctions.

Sotheby's
34–35 New Bond Street
London W1A 2AA England
attn: Press Office

Phillips (New York)   *Phillips, the third large player in the En-*
406 East 79th Street   *glish market (the other two are Christie's*
New York, NY 10021   *and Sotheby's), has yet to hold its first*
(212) 570-4830   *auction on this side of the Atlantic, but*
contact: Marcel Duval   *is exploring the possibility through its*
                                  American representative, Marcel
                                  Duval.

SELLING TO RETAILERS

All things considered, the opportunity for California collectors to sell
their wines back to retailers has been something less than an instant
formula for investment success. Most retailers aren't interested in buy-

ing wine from private individuals. Collectors expect to receive fair market value for their wine. The average retailer has access to stocks of wine at wholesale prices, which usually means he isn't interested in private collections. Friends on the West Coast have related horror stories of fine wines sold to retailers for thirty cents on the dollar, a great deal for wine merchants, but a murderous return for the private seller. However, the law allowing such transactions has been in effect only a short time; perhaps I should wait before passing final judgment.

One gray area, not only in California, but in the rest of the country as well, is whether retailers can operate as agents or brokers for private sales. Select retailers in Los Angeles and San Francisco have been accepting clients' lists on consignment, taking a percentage of the total sale as their commission. The arrangement involves less of a risk on the part of the retailer, and the collector gets a higher return on his wine. In other parts of the country such arrangements are against the law, with two exceptions. In New York, retailers may accept returned wine from clients who originally bought it. And merchants sometimes act as intermediaries between foreign buyers and American collectors.

In the first instance a collector and retailer take advantage of a provision in the New York law which allows a dissatisfied customer to return his wine to the place where he bought it. Of course if several years have elapsed since the original purchase, the wine (assuming it has been stored properly) will have increased considerably in value, a fact reflected in the retailer's "refund" price. In the second situation, a retailer with extensive foreign contacts arranges a sale between an American seller and a willing European buyer. Exporting wine for sale in Europe is easily managed with the assistance of a customs broker, who expedites the necessary paperwork.

Both of these operations presently exist; they are not theoretical, although as they become more common what the attitude of the various states will be is anyone's guess. Depending on the wine, and the strength of the dollar against European currencies, foreign brokers, banks and restaurants sometimes seek to buy wine from Americans. A retailer might be a good way to make contact with one of these firms, or you could discuss a possible sale with the firm directly. Of the English companies listed below, Whitwhams' primary focus is the sale of wine in the U.S.; the other three act as brokers and agents—buying, selling and storing wine for their English clients.

Whitwhams
7 Canal Street
Medford, MA
(617) 391-1233
contact: Linda Uglietti

Old Market Place
Altrincham
Cheshire WA 144 DG England
(061) 928-9416
contact: Timothy Little, Director

Collins Wines
Hawthorn Farm
Great Missenden
  Buckinghamshire HP16 ORL
England
049-783646
contact: Michael Saunders or
  Christopher Collins

Corney and Barrow
29 Rowan Road
London W6 7DT England
01-748-2100
contact: John Armit or Susan
  Depaolis

Brown Brothers
One Duke of York Street
London, SW1Y 6JP England
01-993-6981
contact: M. Brown
New York representative:
  Donald Kurtz
(212) 362-1039

Vinurba, S.A.
1349 Arnex-sur-Orbe
VD Switzerland
024-421170
contact: Robert Magnin,
  Dominique Mottas or Steven
  Burickson

WINE AS A DEDUCTION

Margaux for medical research? Pétrus for PBS? It's not as farfetched as you might think. The fastest way to exploit your IGW's appreciation is to give it away. Donate your wine to charity. Wine lovers from all over the country annually contribute to their favorite charity wine auctions, a particularly Californian approach to raising money for hospitals, public radio and television stations, and other nonprofit enterprises. While it stands to reason that Golden State fund-raisers would center on wine, gifts of appreciable property, such as real estate, art and antiques—and wine—are welcome just about anywhere. A friend of mine donates rare wine to a yearly dinner for a research hospital—and deducts it. Uncle Sam's loss is science's gain.

Giving your wine away won't bring you the same return as selling it. But if you were planning a cash donation to your favorite cause, a gift for the same amount—in wine—can provide double benefits: you reduce what you would have paid in taxes had you sold the wine; at the same time you boost the value of your donation. Generous bidders pushing a given wine to twice its fair market value are so commonplace that appraisers completely disregard charity prices in their calculations.

Since 1985, donors of appreciated property have had to take a little extra trouble when filling out their tax returns. Filers must now notify the IRS of noncash gifts totaling over $500; if the total exceeds $5,000, they must also have the property appraised and provide a brief description of the appraiser's qualifications. Certain people are excluded from appraising your gift (if the gift is wine, for example, the merchant who sold it to you cannot act as your appraiser).

Your accountant or tax attorney should determine the size of your deduction. Your other income, the type of organization you wish to benefit, whether you qualify for the alternative minimum tax and exactly how the beneficiary decides to use your gift will all have a bearing on your final deduction. In the meantime, you can sit back and enjoy the satisfaction of knowing that good taste can serve a good cause.

CHAPTER NINE

BORDEAUX VINEYARDS

I have reached that point in my life where I find it almost impossible to drink an anonymous wine. Wines are not orphans; they have their associations with people, places, history and emotions, all of which subtly enrich our perception of how the wine tastes. The primary goal of wine investing should be pleasure, so the following descriptions try to bring the vineyards to life through some of my personal experiences of nearly three decades as a wine merchant. I have not tried to be historically or technically detailed; other books serve that function far better than I can ever hope to do—I've listed them in the bibliography.

For the most part my production figures have come from *Alexis Lichine's New Encyclopedia of Wines and Spirits*, except in a few instances where first-hand knowledge caused me to modify his figure.

Listing case prices for wines was a far trickier undertaking since enormous regional variation exists in retail pricing practices. California readers may find the prices for French wines to be unusually low, whereas the cost of California wines might strike them as excessively inflated; readers on the East Coast may discover exactly the opposite. I have depended on my own retail records as an indication of price—a practice which at least ensures consistency. The "Open" price indicates what the wine first sold for as futures; the "Now" price indicates what you would most likely have paid for the wine in October 1986 if it were available at a retail outlet. In many cases the "Now" price is a reflection of recent auction prices for the wine, since older vintages of fine wine are often available only at auction.

Group #1 IGW

Château Lafite
(Pauillac)

production: 22,000 cases   first-growth

Lafite is a country vineyard, as opposed to a city vineyard like Mouton.

The trees surrounding a faded yellow château convey the feeling of a country gentleman's farm—a mixture of agriculture and aristocratic formality. Lafite surprised me with its modesty; I expected Buckingham Palace. The interior of the château is designed to a very human scale. A sitting room opens on your right as you enter the house. There's a small formal dining room. A marble staircase leading to the second-floor bedrooms is about as ostentatious as the château gets. Understatement seems the order of the day—in the wine, in the manners of the manager who guided us through the vineyard and in the dignity of the *chais*.

Every time I drink Lafite I'm reminded of the earthen floor of its cellar. Lafite's cellar—as in so many other aspects of the château, including the wine—contrasts dramatically with Mouton's. If Mouton's cellar resembles a church, then Lafite's is closer to a medieval crypt, a rough-hewn subterranean room, dimly lit and floored with earth. The château's oldest vintages are displayed behind the iron bars of a small enclosure off to one side like the aging inhabitants of a sideshow, a nice touch.

My first stay at Lafite was in April of 1981. We were visiting the estate for the express purpose of having a half-dozen nineteenth-century bottles recorked—magnums and double magnums from 1865 and 1870. A few years earlier, I'd shared an 1870 Lafite with two friends. At that time, the early seventies, I hadn't had very many old wines. After opening the bottle I poured each of us a glass and cried "Drink up!" expecting the wine to fade within a matter of minutes. In fact it lasted the course of our entire lunch, convincing me that old wines, if properly maintained, have remarkable staying power.

On the 1981 trip, four of us—my wife, Gloria, my attorney, Eric Rosenthal, his wife-to-be and myself—flew to France with the bottles. During takeoff I rode with the wine belted into the seats on either side of me. After a couple of hours, I began to worry about turbulence, so I carefully set all the bottles in the carpeted legroom space. The stewardess had to coach me up from the floor so I could strap myself in for the approach to Orly.

Eric, the handsome young nephew of Baron Elie de Rothschild, now runs the estate. At the château he informed me that they had no more 1865, so we topped off one bottle with wine from 1870. In a magnanimous gesture of hospitality, the château used a bottle from their own cellar instead of cannibalizing one of my own—at no extra charge. The better part of an entire bottle of 1870 disappeared down the throats of my magnums and double magnums.

I expect 1987 to bring a retrenchment in Bordeaux prices, making this an ideal opportunity to acquire a fine bedrock investment like a case of Lafite.

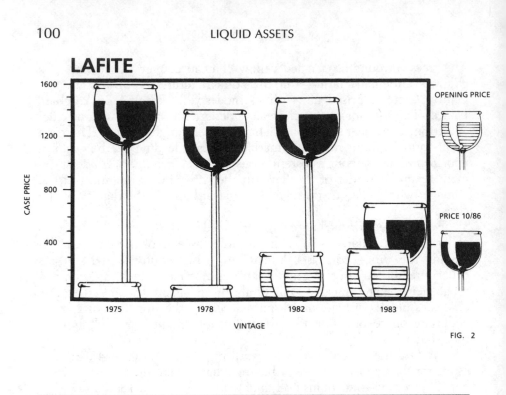

FIG. 2

Château Latour
(Pauillac)

production: 18,000 cases   first-growth

My first experience with Latour was after having visited the vineyard in 1971. The 1970 vintage came to New York in 1972. I saw an article in the *London Times* with the headline "Pollution in the Médoc." There's a Shell refinery located on the Gironde River, within easy distance of all the great châteaux. I thought I'd better look into it. When I visited Latour in 1971 I asked them if they'd had any problems. In the main, they hadn't, but in one section of the vineyard the vines had received a light gray dusting of plastic ash. They seemed to take a fairly casual attitude toward the event, so I didn't worry.

In 1972 I organized a meeting of wine writers and people from the trade. We opened three different bottles of Latour, one from Dreyfus and Ashby, one from Excelsior and one from Austin Nichols. Each bottle had received wine from a different part of the vineyard. My sister had previously commented to me that the Dreyfus and Ashby Latour tasted chemical. I assured her that all young wines had a peculiar taste, but when we tasted all three of the wines together, the Dreyfus and Ashby Latour did indeed seem to taste different.

Alexis Lichine argued that during the youth of a particular vintage there can often be tremendous variation from bottle to bottle. In Latour's case, they were bottling from small oak barrels, now a common practice, but not so at that time. Lichine cryptically commented that the "wine was wearing sleeves." My sister and I remained unconvinced—we thought the bizarre variation in flavor was due to the chemical ash which had fallen on one part of the vineyard.

It transpired that we were wrong. Ten years later I happened to be having lunch at another Bordeaux château when I discovered that the man next to me was a scientist from the Shell refinery. He assured me that the refinery ash hadn't affected the wine, that any chemical quality in the taste of the young wine had probably been due to a recent fertilization in the vineyard, and that shortly after the incident with the ash most of the vineyards had installed pollution counters to monitor local air quality.

Shortly thereafter I tasted all three of the Latours once again. Amazingly, the early variation seemed to have vanished. I also learned that the wines had been bottled over a three-month period, another factor that might have accounted for their different tastes. The experience was a healthy reminder to me that one should never buy on taste alone, or attempt to predict too precisely the future of a wine on the basis of its taste when it's still very young.

Eventually everyone discovers that Latour is the longest-lived of the first-growths, making it one of the most dependable of investments. I can't explain Latour's ability to age; maybe it's the result of the skin contact, maybe the length of time in barrels; perhaps even the soil has a role. In any event, it's the darkest, richest, biggest wine in the Médoc, capable of producing a satisfying wine even in years when other châteaux produce light wine.

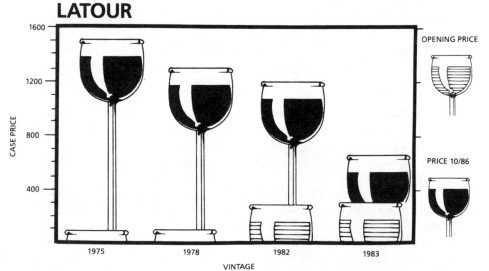

FIG. 3

Château Margaux
(Margaux)

production: 20,000 cases   first-growth

In 1971, I took my son, who was two, and my daughter, who was seven, on a visit to the lower Médoc; one of the places we visited was Margaux. Margaux is a landmark, a formal, colonnaded edifice. Our first sight of Margaux overwhelmed me—a majestic row of columns at the end of a long drive.

As I drew closer, my awe turned to shock: everything was run-down, beaten-up or in disrepair. A dismal atmosphere of ruin permeated the estate, not at all what one expects from a great château. I tasted the 1970, still in the barrel. The impression of decay persisted, even in the *cuverie*.

The next time I saw Margaux was in 1981. I was visiting at Prieuré-Lichine. Alexis Lichine took me over to Margaux while it was still in the process of being restored. Since my last visit, Pierre Ginestet had sold the estate to André Mentzelopoulus. The change was breathtaking. Workers were spreading fresh earth over the vineyards; the château itself had undergone a facelift and the interior now resembled a French salon.

The wines themselves had also changed, mirroring the vigor of the new owners. Most of the wines from the early seventies must be carefully examined for evidence of over-lightness. Margaux is ordinarily a supple wine, but wines from that period seem too light for me. Later wines, on the other hand, beginning with the 1978 and 1979, are outstanding examples of the estate's best efforts. Unfortunately M. Mentzelopoulus died in 1980; his wife, Laura Mentzelopoulus, has continued to produce wines of the same caliber, and has carried on the renovations, initiating a massive program of cellar expansion in 1981.

Margaux has a history of owners with a flair for (not always successful) innovation. Pierre Ginestet imposed very strict standards for the wines in the early sixties. Unless the wine was outstanding he wouldn't declare a vintage. His actions created a stir among other Bordeaux growers, who feared that Ginestet's practice of declaring vintages only in an exceptional year would prove disastrous for sales in average or mediocre years. Cos d'Estournel was the only other vineyard to go along—at that time also owned by the Ginestet family, and the practice was soon abandoned.

A short time ago I found myself at Château Pontet-Canet, participating in a horizontal tasting (different wines, same vintage) of Bordeaux wines from 1980. Three wines stood out: Margaux, Latour and Pichon-Lalande. The 1980s were not much appreciated in this country because it wasn't a "star" vintage. Too bad. For only $20–$25 somebody could get a great experience of a first-growth. I sold dozens of cases of 1980 Margaux in New York. Now there's none left—I can't get anymore.

In 1982 Margaux was one of the vineyards that had problems with "hot" fermentation (fermentation proceeds too quickly, the temperature rises beyond the point at which yeast can survive, and the yeast dies before fermentation can be completed). The estate lost a good percentage of the vintage. The remaining wine made it to bottles, however. It tasted good, still does. If I were to buy wine today and knew nothing about it, I'd buy Margaux—it's a rising star. If Lafite is a bedrock investment, Margaux is a climber.

1975		1978		1982		1983	
OPEN	NOW	OPEN	NOW	OPEN	NOW	OPEN	NOW
$80	$1,200	$80	$900	$300	$1,080	$330	$700

Château Pétrus
(Pomerol)

production: 3,800   unclassified

Nothing about the physical appearance of Château Pétrus would alert you to its status as the producer of the world's most expensive wine. It's small and impeccably maintained, but so are other vineyards in the Pomerol, an area of Bordeaux noted for the small acreage of its estates. In 1974, Pétrus acquired fifteen percent of a contiguous property, Château Gazin, so they could very sparingly increase their production.

Pétrus reminds me of a baseball player with an exceptional agent, a brilliant negotiator capable of parlaying his client's reputation into a salary of several million dollars a year. Are other players as good? Without a doubt. Are their agents as good? Not likely. Pétrus has Jean-Pierre Mouiex, and the rest of the wine world has . . . well, everyone else.

Mouiex is a man of legendary canniness. Before the sixties Pétrus was not a well-known wine. A small coterie of New York diners began bruiting about the name. Over time the wine acquired a cachet that increased in inverse proportion to the size of its production. Through the seventies the price of Pétrus kept pace with the best of the Médoc vineyards—first $200, then $300, then $400 a case. But in 1982 the château broke away from the pack. Pétrus' opening price was almost contemptuously out of proportion to other Bordeaux vineyards—and instead of discouraging sales, the high price seemed to fuel demand. The timing was perfect.

I would stay away from the wine until the price drops—unless you find a discounted case. There's simply no way to justify the present price.

PÉTRUS

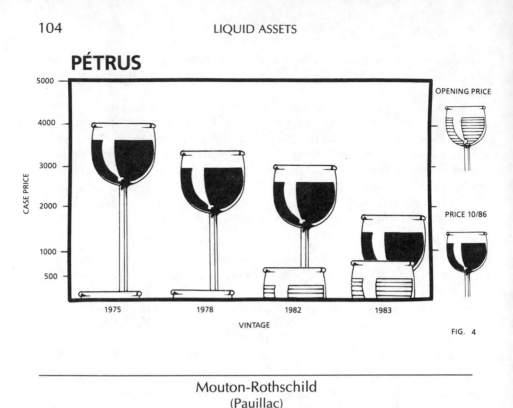

FIG. 4

Mouton-Rothschild
(Pauillac)

production: 22,000 cases   first-growth

Mouton is a library museum. Driving up to it, I had the feeling I was approaching a small government building surrounded by a garden, everything precise and in its place. The formal, but not unfriendly restraint of the employees suggests well-mannered officials rather than vineyard workers. The interior of the château is awash with marble, with paintings, with the high ceilings that connote statelike importance. Overall, there's an overwhelming presence of wealth—more than any château I've ever visited. The château itself is particularly imposing; the manicured lawns, the gardens, *cuverie* and cellar rooms create an impression of money, power, prestige and elegance all in a space much smaller than other renowned châteaux (Margaux, for example). Proof of that power was Mouton's elevation to first-growth status in 1973.

Mouton has not been as dedicated to preserving their old wines as their rival Lafite; oddly, the bottles of 1869 Mouton which I presently own came from Lafite. Recent years have seen a fashion among collectors of rare bottles for vertical collections—all Mouton vintages from 1945 through the present day, for example. I personally know of only four complete collections, fabulously expensive, because of the difficulty of obtaining bottles in the off years like 1950 and 1951.

While I find it difficult to recommend purchasing Mouton at these prices, the wine is so highly regarded as an investment vehicle that even a market hiccup might not reduce prices or make more available. Buy it if you want it.

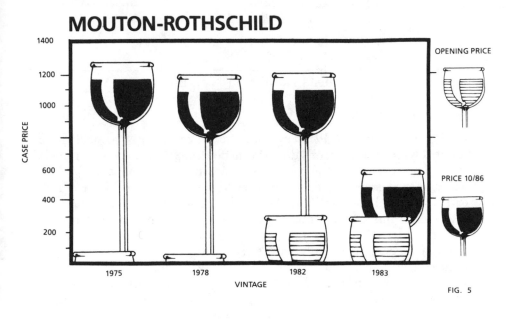

MOUTON-ROTHSCHILD

FIG. 5

Château Haut-Brion
(Graves)

production: 12,000 cases (red)   first-growth
less than 1,000 cases (white)

Haut-Brion's *cuverie* made a strong impression on me when I first visited it in the mid-sixties. The estate had just installed electronically controlled vats of stainless steel. Their methods and equipment struck me as incredibly forward at the time, which raises the question, Why haven't these wines commanded a higher value? All I can surmise is that Haut-Brion's marketing has not kept pace with the other châteaux.

Another odd fact is the conspicuous absence of nineteenth-century wines from this château; I have seen only one Haut-Brion dating from 1899. That exception aside, I have never come across a bottle earlier than the twenties. At a Christie's auction to celebrate the fiftieth anniversary of the estate's ownership by the Dillon family the oldest vintage available was from 1920.

For the standpoint of investment, I'd recommend that wine lovers purchase Haut-Brion starting with the 1985 vintage. In terms of their reputation, I think they've turned a corner, and as the market grows this established first-growth from Graves can only receive more and more attention.

1975		1978		1982		1983	
OPEN	NOW	OPEN	NOW	OPEN	NOW	OPEN	NOW
$78	$1,000	$81	$800	$259	$800	$299	$550

Château La Mission-Haut-Brion
(Graves)

production: 4,800 cases   Cru Classé

During the summer of 1971 my family and I rented a house in Pyla, a resort town about an hour's drive from Bordeaux. On weekdays I made it my business to visit a couple of châteaux each day, tasting their wines, meeting as many people as I could. One afternoon I knocked off early, seduced by a small nine-hole golf course almost within the Bordeaux city limits. I was then (and still remain) an avid golfer. The course bordered La Mission and I gazed over at a vineyard planted, somewhat unconventionally, not only with vines, but with roses. Intrigued, I visited the château the next day with my wife and children, where I heard that Henri Woltner, the owner of La Mission from 1924 until his death fifty years later, had planted the roses as an experiment, wondering if the rose bouquet would somehow work its way into his wine.

Even if the roses do not translate directly into a rose-flavored wine, Woltner was certainly an innovative proprietor. La Mission was the first Bordeaux estate to use glass-lined steel tanks. Other châteaux have since installed stainless steel tanks, relying on water running down the outside of the tanks to cool the fermenting wine. La Mission's tanks seem to perform quite well without the water.

Several years ago Henri Woltner's daughter and son-in-law, Monsieur and Madame Francis Woltner-Dewavrin, sold the estate. They have since devoted themselves to their interests in Woltner Winery in California. They were the generous sort of proprietors dear to a merchant's heart; during a visit in 1975, which coincided with a visit by Ab Simon, president of Château and Estate, the wine importing arm of Seagram's, they threw me a surprise birthday party, complete with cake, candles and—as one would expect in Bordeaux—red wine.

The wine from La Mission-Haut-Brion seems to hold itself aloof from all the blather about nouveau vinification and accessibility. In their youth, these wines can be hard, tannic and concentrated, not at all immediately appealing. In time they become intense, complicated wines of outstanding value, a style unlikely to change with the new owners, the Dillon family, of Haut-Brion fame.

1975		1978		1982		1983	
OPEN	NOW	OPEN	NOW	OPEN	NOW	OPEN	NOW
$70	$1,500	$65	$660	$240	$580	$265	$520

Château Pichon-Lalande
(Pauillac)

production: 17,500 cases   second-growth

Pichon reminds me of Château Margaux in that an improvement in the quality of the wine coincided with an upgrading of the vineyard and its equipment. Mme. de Lencquesaing, the administrator of the estate, and her husband both travel extensively to promote Pichon's wines. Also, like Margaux, she uses Professor Emile Peynaud as a consulting oenologist.

In the spring of 1983 Mme. Lencquesaing arrived unannounced in my New York shop. She sputtered and fumed about Robert Parker, Jr., who had condemned her 1982 Pichon without ever visiting the château. Instead he had telephoned the cellarmaster, who quite candidly admitted that they were having problems with a "hot" fermentation. Rather than taste the wine, in order to determine whether or not the château had successfully overcome its problem, he had simply consigned the wine to his "no buy" list. She waxed livid for a few moments, finally calming down when I told her that I had always enjoyed her wines, and that in any event I didn't have anything to do with Parker or his reviews.

Ultimately the situation was straightened out. Parker reevaluated the wines, wrote that they had conquered the fermentation problem and gave the 1982 Pichon his endorsement.

1975		1978		1982		1983	
OPEN	NOW	OPEN	NOW	OPEN	NOW	OPEN	NOW
$39	$600	$45	$500	$136	$600	$290	$400

Château Léoville-Las-Cases
(St.-Julien)

production: 30,000 cases   second-growth

Léoville-Las-Cases is adjacent to Latour, somewhat surrounded by Beychevelle, Talbot and Pichon-Longueville. Overlooking the Gironde, its position calls to mind the Bordeaux saying that vineyards with a river view make the best wine. Many critics have given Lascases the title of the "poor man's Latour"—both wines are big and fleshy, becoming subtle after long aging. Presently the wine is enjoying a vogue. As I mentioned earlier, when clients of mine can't afford first-growths, they usually go for one of three wines, Pichon-Lalande, Ducru-Beaucaillou and Léoville-Las-Cases.

Despite its high production, there's never enough Las-Cases around. The policy of the estate's administrator, Michel Delon, may have contributed to this impression by his admitted strategy of releasing the wine in smaller amounts than the other châteaux, keeping a close watch on prices.

1975		1978		1982		1983	
OPEN	NOW	OPEN	NOW	OPEN	NOW	OPEN	NOW
$38	$550	$39	$480	$134	$600	$190	$420

Château Ausone
(St.-Émilion)

production: 2,000 cases   Premier Grand Cru (A)

Ausone was the first château I visited during my first visit to Bordeaux in 1962. What I saw was an old run-down house and cellar. I bought several magnums of 1955 Ausone to take home with me. It borders on Château Belair, which has the same owner, and the two estates share a single cellar. An apocryphal story connects the estate to the vacation residence of the Roman poet Ausonious, who ostensibly visited the area to avail himself of the aphrodisiac powers of a local spring.

In recent times Ausone seems to be following in a path blazoned by Pétrus. Limited production, a demanding market and opening prices higher than Lafite are turning Ausone into an expensive "cult" wine. At the present level of pricing I'd be very wary of extensive purchases for investment.

1975		1978		1982		1983	
OPEN	NOW	OPEN	NOW	OPEN	NOW	OPEN	NOW
$60	$800	$65	$990	$540	$1,500	$590	$790

Château Cheval Blanc
(St.-Émilion)

production: 11,500 cases   Premier Grand Cru (A)

Cheval Blanc is one of the few first-growths to have remained in the hands of the same family since its inception. That sort of continuity is invaluable when it comes to establishing a wine's reputation. In 1980 I read several writers' comments about the 1947 Cheval Blanc, which they described as the "wine of the century." My curiosity was piqued, so I bought a bottle and tasted it. Frankly, the taste was less than overwhelming. To me the wine seemed faded, suggestive perhaps of a former complexity, but definitely past its prime. About a year later in Paris I encountered an old collector who wanted to sell twenty-five cases of the 1947. The bottles were in an unacceptable disarray: some of the labels were faded; they needed new corks and cases. After my recent experience tasting the "wine of the century" I only agreed to the sale on the condition that the collector first send the bottles back to the château for recorking, fresh labels and new cases. The renewal process took almost a year.

We took delivery of the wine in New York in 1982 and over the course of the year sold each case for $3,200; the present value of a case of 1947 is around $5,400, if you can find any. Collectors who've drunk their purchases tell me the wine is delicious, an argument perhaps for the preservative power of Parisian cellars over their American counterparts.

In the right vintage, Cheval Blanc can be the most outstanding wine in Bordeaux—round, supple, harmonious, with an unbelievably long finish. The 1964, a poor vintage in Bordeaux generally, was a wonderful wine at Cheval Blanc. As a wine merchant I have an obligation to taste many wines in the course of my business—too many— and I've always denied myself the pleasure of buying wine for my own home, because of the wasted tasting opportunity. Cheval Blanc has been my one exception to the rule. I recently bought several cases of 1964 Cheval Blanc at Christie's Chicago auction for $1,200 a case.

1975		1978		1982		1983	
OPEN	NOW	OPEN	NOW	OPEN	NOW	OPEN	NOW
$90	$900	$80	$1,200	$259	$1,000	$320	$600

Group #2 IGW

Château Palmer
(Margaux)

production: 11,000 cases   third-growth

Palmer combines great wine with great marketing. An easy name, a distinctive black label lettered in gold, and a superb wine with a history of superior vintages in the sixties and seventies have all made Palmer a good investment value. Today several commercial firms have an interest in the estate, the English one represented by Peter Sichel perhaps the most visible. Sichel is a lean, soft-spoken, scholarly man who typifies for me the refined Bordeaux winemaker. Under the present ownership the prices of Palmer have risen to first-growth levels, despite the estate's official third-growth classification.

I recall one spectacular evening at the château, the food overshadowed by the wines. Sichel had arranged a blind tasting of wine which he asked the guests to identify. The wines were later revealed to be 1952, 1953 and 1955 Lafite. Sichel's confidence in his own wine may be measured by the fact that he later served us the 1962 Palmer, a rich, supple wine that showed very favorably by comparison with the Lafites.

My attitude toward investing in Palmer is very optimistic. There's plenty of it around and it has a high price, suggesting that its present popularity has a more solid basis than simply fashion, and as a glance at the prices below demonstrates, it appreciates quite rapidly.

1975		1978		1982		1983	
OPEN	NOW	OPEN	NOW	OPEN	NOW	OPEN	NOW
$55	$700	$65	$560	$240	$660	$260	$500

Château Lynch-Bages
(Pauillac)

production: 22,000 cases   fifth-growth

André Cazes, the owner of Lynch-Bages, and I once sat next to each other at a lunch given by Lafite. Preceding the lunch a group of people in the wine trade, proprietors, *négociants* and merchants, had sampled a selection of recently bottled 1981s. The samples were numbered, their identities concealed, so we had to make our selections exclusively on taste. My two choices were both wines I recognized and loved, Latour and Peyrabon, both from opposite ends of the price spectrum.

I no longer recall the choices of M. Cazes, but upon hearing my selections he immediately agreed that the 1981 Peyrabon was a very good wine, especially in its price range. He also informed me that his own goal was to produce great wine that people could afford to drink. Great wine that people can afford to drink pretty much sums up Lynch-Bages. Problems with history prevent Lynch from being the equal of the big three (Pichon, Ducru, Lascases) that wine lovers inevitably buy when they don't want to pay quite the price of the first-growths. Still, it's a very good wine which deserves elevation to second-growth status. A recent testimony to its popularity may be found in a Gault-Millau magazine poll of wine specialists; they accorded Lynch-Bages a perfect 100, promoting it to first-growth rank ahead of all other Bordeaux except Haut-Batailley and Grand-Puy-Lacoste.

1975		1978		1982		1983	
OPEN	NOW	OPEN	NOW	OPEN	NOW	OPEN	NOW
$29	$440	$39	$360	$124	$380	$175	$320

Château Beychevelle
(St.-Julien)

production: 26,000 cases   fourth-growth

Beychevelle not only has one of the few genuine châteaux in Bordeaux, dating from 1757, rather than the nineteenth century, but there's also a charming legend concerning the origin of its name. As Clive Coates tells the story in his book, *Claret,* ships passing in the Gironde lowered their sails as a token of respect to the sixteenth-century owner, the Duc d'Épernon, who was appointed Admiral of France in 1587. *"Baisse voile,"* French for "lower sails," was *"bêche velle"* in the local Gascon dialect. Coates points out that recent research suggests that the admiral may never have lived on the property, although he still holds out some hope for lovers of apocrypha: the boats may have had to lower their sails in order to stop for customs inspectors or tax collectors.

Beychevelle was once much larger than its present 173 acres, including much land devoted to farming. Pierre-François Guestier, one of the founding partners in the firm Barton and Guestier, purchased the estate in 1825 and actually started a cork plantation. Wheat is still grown on Beychevelle property and a herd of cows provides the vineyard with a ready supply of organic fertilizer.

Like many of the vineyards I've selected as IGW, Beychevelle immediately gives a sense of being maintained by people who care. Meticulous attention to detail in the château, gardens and outbuildings suggests an attitude that's bound to show up in the wine. My own experiences of young Beychevelle have been of big, leathery wines that need time to mature. Other wine writers disagree, having discovered an early suppleness that has eluded my own tasting. A point on which everyone agrees is the inaccuracy of the wine's present classification: it should be placed in the second rank. Moreover, a look at the appreciation for previous vintages shows a wine with serious investment potential at an affordable price.

1975		1978		1982		1983	
OPEN	NOW	OPEN	NOW	OPEN	NOW	OPEN	NOW
$35	$360	$42	$320	$126	$310	$140	$290

Château Trotanoy
(Pomerol)

production: 2,500 cases   unclassified

Trotanoy, with its tiny production so typical of Pomerol, and its relatively recent reputation, is often overlooked by wine writers who like to concentrate on more legendary châteaux of Bordeaux. The comments which do exist are intriguing nevertheless. The "Bible of Bordeaux wines," as Féret's *Bordeaux and Its Wines* likes to bill itself, uses identical language to describe the bouquet of both Pétrus and Trotanoy: "a very pronounced fragrance of truffles." Since the comments in Féret have been solicited from the proprietors, and Jean-Pierre Mouiex has an interest in both vineyards, I shouldn't be surprised to see the wines described similarly.

Alexis Lichine devotes a mere half dozen lines to it in his *Encyclopedia of Wines and Spirits,* but he mentions that the wine is made from old vines, and in his courageous attempt to rectify the classification of 1855 he elevates Trotanoy to the status of "Cru Exceptionnel," a designation roughly equivalent to second-growth in the older order.

David Peppercorn affirms the stylistic similarity between Pétrus and Trotanoy, a comparison born out by the increase in price of recent vintages. I'm convinced Trotanoy will prove to be a good long-term investment (look at what's happened to the 1975), but present prices are so high that the likelihood of being able to turn the wine within five years for a significant gain over your purchase price is not good. Wait for the prices to come down, or get a deal on an early futures price before buying.

1975		1978		1982		1983	
OPEN	NOW	OPEN	NOW	OPEN	NOW	OPEN	NOW
$39	$660	$54	$590	$234	$720	$299	$500

Château Cos d'Estournel
(St.-Estèphe)

production: 25,000 cases   second-growth

In the early seventies I hosted a weekly radio show called *Wine and Other Things* on WNCN. Robert Mondavi and Alexis Lichine were two of my early guests, as was a young, aristocratic man who was just starting to make wine at Cos d'Estournel. His name was Bruno Prats.

From 1919 until 1971 Cos was the property of the famous Ginestet family, and was most recently administered by Bernard Ginestet. When financial difficulties caused many of the Ginestet holdings to be broken up, Cos went to Bernard's aunt, Madame Prats. Her son, Bruno, now runs the estate. I recall Bruno Prats as an elegant, highly informed young man who defended Cos as an example of the older style of Bordeaux wines. On the face of it, his wines indicate a change of heart; Cos of the eighties drinks much sooner than vintages two decades earlier.

Prats does an admirable job as *explicateur* and publicist for the new style of Bordeaux wines. In a recent interview with *The Wine Spectator* he took pains to point out the role of Emile Peynaud in defining and changing the way wine has been made, not only at Cos, but all over Bordeaux. A philosophy with which Prats obviously agrees: "traditionalists say that in the old days, the wines were hard, but they kept well; today, they are so supple they will never hold up. I'll take that bet, if only because I don't believe that one must have a detestable character in childhood to have a likable one as an adult."

1975		1978		1982		1983	
OPEN	NOW	OPEN	NOW	OPEN	NOW	OPEN	NOW
$36	$380	$45	$360	$120	$480	$180	$290

Château La Lagune
(Haut-Médoc)

production: 25,000 cases   third-growth

Nathaniel Johnston, the agent for La Lagune, escorted Gloria and me through the vineyard in 1964. Although this was my first visit to the estate, I wasn't a complete stranger to the wine. I had bought the 1960 La Lagune for $14 a case, selling it for $1.99 a bottle. The wine had inspired quite a bit of customer loyalty, which was what prompted my visit to the château.

Johnston made an emphatic tour guide. I was too new to the wine trade to recognize in the ultramodern fermentation tanks one of the restoration success stories of the Médoc. It all seemed rather science-fiction-like at the time, with Johnston emphasizing the importance of sanitation and drawing my attention to the stainless steel pipes which fed wine from the fermenting tanks to the the oak casks. Only in retrospect, after logging many more hours on estates nowhere near so meticulous, was I able to appreciate what I had seen.

Georges Brunet, the architect of this transformation, no longer owns La Lagune. An overoptimistic prediction of the size of the 1961 harvest prompted him to sell *sur souche*, that is, still on the vine. When the harvest was smaller than expected, he was forced to sell out. M. Borie, of the Ayala champagne firm, became the new owner. Judging by the wine, M. Borie continued in the vein commenced by his predecessor; his widow now runs the vineyard.

La Lagune is often spoken of as wine whose staying power is more a part of its nineteenth-century reputation than present-day reality, perhaps because so many of the vines were replanted under M. Brunet. In my experience this isn't quite accurate. I've sold both 1961s and 1962s in my shop. Wine lovers expect the 1961s to last, which they have; but friends still surprise me with the 1962s I sold them twenty years ago. The fairly remarkable gains shown below indicate that I'm not alone in my convictions about the life of this wine.

1975		1978		1982		1983	
OPEN	NOW	OPEN	NOW	OPEN	NOW	OPEN	NOW
$27	$320	$29	$310	$124	$320	$160	$260

Château Cantemerle
(Haut-Médoc)

production: 20,000 cases   fifth-growth

Descriptions of Cantemerle inevitably focus on its ridiculously inappropriate classification as a fifth-growth, and the taste of the wine more than justifies the observation. Although La Lagune and Cantemerle are barely a half mile apart, their wines are as unlike each other as apples and oranges. Where La Lagune is firm, straight to the point, Cantemerle is languorous, even soft.

As a merchant I've had a great deal of success with this wine. The 1961 sold very well although the wine was a virtual unknown in New York. As late as the summer of 1971 I could still go to the château and arrange to buy several hundred cases each of the wonderful 1964s and 1966s. My importer delayed forwarding the check to the château agent, an imposition that cost me one hundred cases in each vintage. Both vintages sold out within six weeks of their arrival in my shop, an unusually fast disappearance for those days.

As an investment Cantemerle is a sleeping giant. The wines of the seventies failed to impress me in the way that their precursors of the previous decade had, but the eighties have seen some spectacularly good wines, both the 1982 and the exceptional 1983, considered one of the top wines of the vintage. In 1981 the firm of Cordier took over the running of the vineyard, after its sale to an insurance group. Cordier intends to expand the vineyard acreage under cultivation, evidenced by the production figure of 20,000 cases, provided by Alexis Lichine, more than double the previous decades' annual output of 6,000 to 8,000 cases.

As market pressure forces prices of Ducru, Pichon-Lalande and Léoville-Las-Cases ever higher, Cantemerle will be more and more recognized as the undervalued wine of the Haut-Médoc. The futures price of the 1983 opened at $120 per case; at the moment (September, 1986) I'd be surprised if you could find it anyplace in New York for less than $220–$260.

1975		1978		1982		1983	
OPEN	NOW	OPEN	NOW	OPEN	NOW	OPEN	NOW
$27	$260	$26	$290	$80	$240	$122	$210

Domaine de Chevalier
(Graves)

production: 5,000 cases   Grand Cru

Domaine de Chevalier is the Third Musketeer in the investment trio that also includes La Lagune and Cantemerle, wines with recognized histories of excellence whose trading stature is just beginning to reflect their true value. Domaine is a wine with a strong English market, but is a relatively unknown wine in the U.S., a fact I can only attribute to its modest refusal to follow the Bordeaux practice of aggrandizing its name with "Château." "Domaine" isn't a recognizable term to many wine lovers, nor does it fire the popular imagination with visions of exclusivity or sophistication in the way that "Château" (however erroneously) might.

In fact, Domaine de Chevalier seems to have accommodated itself to modern tastes very little. Michel Dovaz, author of the *Encyclopedia of the Great Wines of Bordeaux*, points out that Domaine wines undergo an unusually long fermentation and maceration, at the very minimum lasting three weeks, in order to extract the maximum fruit flavors from the grapes. But, as he further observes, the practice results in wines whose long aging sometimes prompts frustrated wine lovers to drink them too young. Domaine has since built an extra cellar for bottle storage in order to ensure that a representative share of its wines manages to last until their prime. The white wine of Domaine de Chevalier is also extremely long-lived, although available in such small supply (600 cases annually) that it's almost a cult item.

Michael Broadbent gave the status of Domaine a boost when he announced that the 1979 was his favorite wine of that year. Subsequent vintages have risen dramatically in price and we can expect to pay even higher prices for good vintages in the near future.

1975		1978		1982		1983	
OPEN	NOW	OPEN	NOW	OPEN	NOW	OPEN	NOW
$28	$290	$36	$320	$140	$260	$200	$240

Château Ducru-Beaucaillou
(St.-Julien)

production: 15,000 cases   second-growth

The spectacular château at Ducru makes it difficult to believe that this wine hasn't had an unbroken record of quality production for at least a century and a half. But in fact, the fortunes of the Nathaniel Johnston firm, which had owned the estate since 1866, suffered a decline in the decade before the Second World War, and Ducru suffered as well. The restoration of the wine to the prestige and glory befitting a second-growth began with François Borie, who bought the estate in 1941. The estate passed to his son, Jean-Eugène Borie, in 1953, and has seen nothing but an increase in stature and price, especially since the early seventies.

Ducru illustrates what can happen when a dilapidated estate with old vines receives the sort of continuous care and promotion it deserves. The physical layout of Ducru is magisterial; the château suggests the sort of aristocratic wine associated with Borie's northern neighbors, Lafite and Latour. For almost thirty years Borie has diligently pursued a standard of winemaking to match this expectation, with the price reward that such dedication brings.

Ducru is hardly undiscovered wine. Wine lovers expect great wines from this estate and seem willing to pay near first-growth prices for good vintages. Stay away from the 1982; I think the price is presently too high and the market will ultimately correct it.

1975		1978		1982		1983	
OPEN	NOW	OPEN	NOW	OPEN	NOW	OPEN	NOW
$50	$420	$55	$480	$138	$640	$200	$310

Château Figeac
(St.-Émilion)

production: 17,000 cases   Premier Grand Cru

I do not know Thierry Manoncourt personally, although he made such an impression on me when he was once pointed out at a wine function we both attended that when I was putting together this book I nearly went mad trying to find a reference to the "Baron" Thierry Manoncourt. He looked like an aristocrat and I was sure he was one.

Figeac and Cheval Blanc were once part of the same estate and Figeac has maintained a reputation for elegance among the ranks of St.-Émilion wines, typically more celebrated for their warmth and accessibility. Wine writers who comment on St.-Émilion's propensity for producing good wines in poor years often cite Figeac for their examples: David Peppercorn calls attention to the 1958; and Clive Coates recalls that the 1968 was the only St.-Émilion that year worthy of the Grand Cru Classé appellation. (In St.-Émilion wines are tasted annually, and if not meeting the standard, denied the right to use their classification on the label.)

Figeac's prices in the last several years have struck me as inflated. Notice the opening difference between the 1978 and the 1982. But there has been some correction; the 1985 (a good year) mercifully opened lower than the 1984 (a poor one). The price of Figeac has sometimes seemed foolishly high to me (as has Ducru's). Given the choice of buying a drinkable 1979 or 1981 in a better growth, I have to ask myself, why should I pay more for an immature inferior one? Don't misunderstand me: Figeac makes very good wine; in a good year, the equal of Cheval Blanc. I just think that its price, for the moment, has gotten out of control.

1975		1978		1982		1983	
OPEN	NOW	OPEN	NOW	OPEN	NOW	OPEN	NOW
$38	$360	$29	$390	$195	$420	$230	$340

Group #3 IGW

Château La Grave-Trigant-de-Boisset
(Pomerol)

production: 2,000 cases   unclassified

My experience with La Grave dates only from the seventies, when the Bouché family sold it to the Mouiex family. Christian Mouiex, son of Jean-Pierre, now runs the estate. The younger Mouiex is a man of movie-star good looks combined with an unexpected modesty. In May of 1986 we met at a function in New York. I recounted how some friends and family had recently come together at dinner to celebrate my wife's birthday and we had drunk three wines from 1979: Pétrus, La Grave and a B.V. Georges de Latour Cabernet. Mouiex looked shocked when I told him that the favorite had been La Grave. I thought the wine was fabulous.

He disagreed, conceding only that as each year passed he was able to slowly improve the wine. Perhaps the family experience with Pétrus has bred a certain caution into him. After all, the wine will certainly be compared to Pétrus, and any attempt to inflate its value would be perceived as grandstanding.

In my own opinion, Christian is producing great wine whose value is presently underestimated. I've sold the wine since 1976 and I expect that it will go the route of Cantemerle, La Lagune and Gloria, estates that were once unknown in this country and are now doing quite well.

1975		1978		1982		1983	
OPEN	NOW	OPEN	NOW	OPEN	NOW	OPEN	NOW
$18	$360	$25	$280	$80	$400	$90	$280

Château La Gaffelière
(St.-Émilion)

production: 10,000 cases   Premier Grand Cru

La Gaffelière is a wine I encountered in the most prosaic of wine merchant fashions; I tasted the 1964 in my shop while looking for a representative St.-Émilion. The wine floored me. It had a penetrating flavor
of fruit with a long, long finish. Like many wines from St.-Émilion it
has a high percentage of Merlot, giving it a mouth-filling lushness in
its best years. I was instantly drugged by its loveliness.

La Gaffelière sometimes suffers from inconsistency. I've sold it as
an upper-class wine with a middle-class price for almost twenty years.
The price of the wine shot up with the 1981, which the *New York
Times* dubbed the wine of the vintage in St.-Émilion. I place it among
the #3 IGW because it has great potential, but has not yet achieved
the recognition necessary to pump the price through the roof.

1975		1978		1982		1983	
OPEN	NOW	OPEN	NOW	OPEN	NOW	OPEN	NOW
$30	$290	$29	$280	$117	$240	$140	$220

Château Gruaud-Larose
(St.-Julien)

production: 22,000 cases   second-growth

That Gruaud is owned by the shipping firm of Cordier suggests two
things: up-to-date technology and old-world skills. And in fact, that's
not an inappropriate description of the estate today. The château, built
in modern times, sits at the end of a dirt road off the main highway. A
deceptive eighteenth-century atmosphere hangs about the estate—a herd
of cows supplies Gruaud and Talbot, another Cordier estate, with manure for fertilizer—but a peek inside the impeccable *cuverie* reveals modern stainless steel vats.

George Pauli is the young and able winemaker for Cordier. After
we met him in the city of Bordeaux in the summer of 1981, he took
Gloria and myself on a picnic at Château Meyney, another Cordier
property, where we spent a great lunch in the open air discussing Cordier wines. From the standpoint of investment strategy, it makes sense
to buy Gruaud. In their efforts to lend distinctive characters to both
Talbot and Gruaud, Cordier seems to be emphasizing Gruaud's elegance
on the one hand, and Talbot's solidity on the other. This distinction
has manifested itself in a widening gap between the prices in the two
wines, growing from five percent to twenty percent in the last five years.

1975		1978		1982		1983	
OPEN	NOW	OPEN	NOW	OPEN	NOW	OPEN	NOW
$36	$290	$27	$280	$122	$240	$140	$220

Château Canon
(St.-Émilion)

production: 7,500 cases   Premier Grand Cru

Canon is a perplexing wine, a good example perhaps of how word of mouth among wine enthusiasts triggers an increase in popularity. The wine came to my attention several years ago because so many of my clients who regularly buy first-growths began appending two or three cases of Canon on to their orders. Why? What was going on? Since 1982 a small group of St.-Émilion and Pomerol wines have been slipping onto the board—Vieux Certan, Canon, l'Évangile and l'Arrosée, recommended by clients who want a good value. In this case, the sophistication of the buyers is a good endorsement.

1975		1978		1982		1983	
OPEN	NOW	OPEN	NOW	OPEN	NOW	OPEN	NOW
$28	$290	$36	$360	$120	$380	$130	$240

Château Grand-Puy-Lacoste
(Pauillac)

production: 14,000 cases   fifth-growth

Jean-Eugène Borie, the proprietor of Ducru-Beaucaillou, bought this very dilapidated château in 1978. I remember visiting the estate shortly before Borie purchased it. I couldn't believe this decrepit château and ill-kempt vineyard were the stuff of a classified growth. A few months later I ran into Henri Martin, proprietor of Château Gloria, who mentioned that his good friend Borie had recently bought a controlling interest in Grand-Puy-Lacoste. I remember thinking, "What a sucker!" and wondering if he had seen the vineyard.

My judgment was premature, unduly influenced perhaps by the state of the château. Of course the fabulous Borie magic has turned the vineyard around entirely, although the château itself remains derelict. The running of the estate is now the responsibility of his son and daughter-in-law, Xavier and Monique Borie. In 1980 I paid a second visit to the estate and found it utterly transformed, a change reflected in the wine almost immediately upon the change of ownership. The 1978 was a highly tannic wine in the old-fashioned style. In a 1982 tasting Clives

Coates noted that the 1978 still needed a good ten years. Borie involvement in the wine is a sure guarantee of future quality offerings.

1975		1978		1982		1983	
OPEN	NOW	OPEN	NOW	OPEN	NOW	OPEN	NOW
$30	$360	$24	$300	$119	$380	$140	$240

Château Gloria
(St.-Julien)

production: 17,000 cases   Cru Bourgeois

Gloria is a tribute to the dedication and hard work of Henri Martin,
the arch-conservative former mayor of St. Julien. Patched together from
bits and pieces of other nearby vineyards—Gruaud Larose, Duhart-Milon,
Léoville-Poyferré and St.-Pierre—the estate was assembled as Martin
could afford to buy each parcel. In his book *The Winemasters* Nicolas
Faith says that the visionary proprietor lived on the second floor of his
chais, denying himself even the luxury of carpeting as long as there
remained land to be bought.

Mutual friends introduced us in 1970. He is a man who knows how
to live through tough times, as the early seventies were for him. In late
1972 I visited the estate and found such a glut of wine that he had
filled an empty swimming pool with the overflow of cases. As a result
of that meeting I bought several hundred cases of his 1966 and 1970,
which I sold in New York for $50 and $60 a case respectively. Once in
a while I'll encounter a case of the 1966 that somebody's saved; it goes
for $300 today, still not a bad buy. The 1975 and 1978 have kept pace
with their classified "betters," appreciating to almost ten times their
opening prices.

Gloria is an inexpensive wine, even today, despite the periodic shot
in the arm it gets from wine critics. I have a special affection for it
because I introduced it to New York. As an investment it's almost too
inexpensive to pass up—a true liquid asset, and there's always the possibility that someone will come along and market the hell out of it.

1975		1978		1982		1983	
OPEN	NOW	OPEN	NOW	OPEN	NOW	OPEN	NOW
$24	$220	$26	$240	$70	$160	$70	$100

Château Rausan-Ségla
(Margaux)

production: 11,000 cases   second-growth

My decision to include Rausan-Ségla as the last investment-grade red
wine from Bordeaux is a reminder that reputation *and* quality must go

hand in hand if a wine is ultimately to achieve the prestige to make it a good investment. For most of the twentieth century Rausan was in the hands of a branch of the Cruze family, the Bordeaux *négociants*. It changed hands in 1956 and then again in 1960, when it became the property of the present owners, the British firm of John Holt. Since Holt had no experience in making wine, it is perhaps wise that he turned over the administration to another of his purchases, the Bordeaux firm of Eschenauer.

Rausan is a bargain second-growth, and recent vintages indicate a revival of previous quality. The 1975 was considered an outstanding wine in its classification for the year, and vintages since then have been well received. What the wine presently lacks is a marketing push to bring it to the attention of quality-conscious investors.

1975		1978		1982		1983	
OPEN	NOW	OPEN	NOW	OPEN	NOW	OPEN	NOW
$36	$220	$27	$260	$114	$186	$135	$160

CHAPTER TEN

CALIFORNIA VINEYARDS AND WINERIES

Any purported wine expert who relegates California wines to second-class status has lost touch with reality. By almost any standard—including price—the fine wines of California equal their European competition, including their ability to appreciate in value, as Figures 6 and 7 make clear. Several dramatically publicized tastings, most notably those organized by Stephen Spurrier in 1976 and 1986, have established that even the most partisan advocates of French vineyards are incapable of distinguishing between their own national produce and the best of California.

What California vineyards lack is history. As I've already pointed out, how the public views a wine is as important a determinant of a wine's investment value as its actual taste, maybe even more so. California is beginning to develop its heroes and its legendary wines. Among wine lovers it's more and more common to hear about the discovery

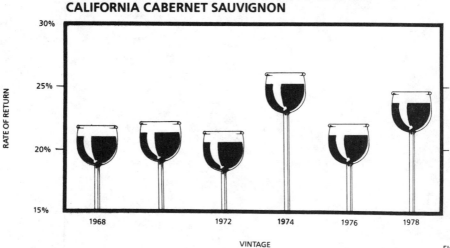

AVERAGE ANNUAL RATES OF RETURN BY VINTAGE CALIFORNIA CABERNET SAUVIGNON

RATE OF RETURN

VINTAGE

FIG 6

RATES OF RETURN RESULTS BY WINERY
CALIFORNIA CABERNET SAUVIGNON

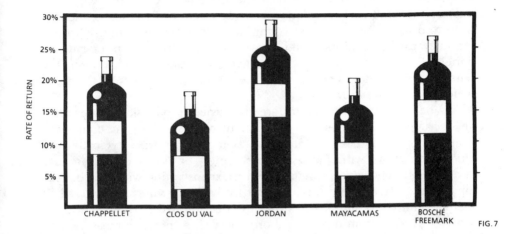

FIG. 7

and consumption of a rare California bottle described in the rapturous language once reserved for the great Bordeaux châteaux.

But whereas the reputation of a French wine seems somehow connected with the château, rooted in the soil of the vineyard, the esteem for an American wine may be a more fickle affair, dependent on a particular winemaker or the driving enthusiasm of a winery owner. If one or the other of these individuals leaves then the wine may suffer a temporary fall from grace—completely independent of the issue of its quality. Fashion plays a stronger role on this side of the Atlantic.

For this reason the prices of California wines may be more volatile than those from France. Many West Coast wineries have established lofty reputations after a single release (Château Montelena, for example), an inconceivable event for a small French or Italian vineyard.

The California wine trade has taken the past two decades to make its vinifying mistakes—the wines are now not so wild, so excessive (remember all those monster Zinfandels of the mid-seventies?). As production costs continue to rise, the next decade will see a consolidation of vineyard ownership; the explosion of boutique vineyards will abate as it becomes less and less possible to make competitive wines on a shoestring.

What follows are some of my impressions of vineyards and wineries with investment potential. The anecdotes are shorter because my experience with the principals in the California wine trade is necessarily shorter than with the proprietors and winemakers of France, and in the scheme of things California is always offering newcomers. In my opinion, these are the vineyards of the future.

Pricing and production notes: Although more and more California wines are sold as futures, especially within the state itself, the following opening prices reflect the cost to the consumer when the wine was released to retail outlets. Winemakers are aware of Americans' inclination to drink their wines too young; as a defensive measure, a winery or vineyard may hold its wine for a year or two longer than a Bordeaux vineyard. In some cases, as long as five years may elapse between the vintage and its retail appearance. The "Now" price refers to the retail value of the wine in March of 1987.

Where California vineyards are concerned, production figures are a less accurate measurement for investment purposes than the equivalent statistics for a Bordeaux château. A Bordeaux vineyard typically produces one or two wines; an American winery or vineyard may produce a dozen different wines, ranging from inexpensive jug wine all the way up to special reserve bottlings. Except for boutique vineyards with small outputs limited to one or two wines, production figures should be taken only as an indication of vineyard or winery size—not as a measurement of IGW output. The production figures for this section derive, in the main, from Anthony Dias Blue's excellent reference, *American Wine* (New York: Doubleday, 1985).

#1 IGW

Beaulieu Vineyard
(Napa)
wine: Cabernet Sauvignon, Georges de Latour, Private Reserve
production: under 10,000 cases

If California vineyards are today producing more quality Cabernets than one wine lover can possibly hope to follow, then a great deal of the blame must laid at the door of B.V. A generation of winemakers has grown up admiring the beautifully structured red wines of André Tchelistcheff, the winemaker at Beaulieu for almost forty years.

Winemakers and vineyards need time to grow, to make mistakes and learn from them. Out of such history comes the control and understanding which produce good wines year in, year out. Continuous ownership by the de Latour family and the devotion of Tchelistcheff allowed B.V. time to develop; perhaps no modern winery, considering the present cost of land and production, will have that luxury.

The signature wine of the vineyard—and the only one to consider for investment purposes—is the Georges de Latour Private Reserve Cabernet, a deep, concentrated wine with the sort of staying power that used to be associated almost exclusively with red Bordeaux. I particularly remember the 1979, an intense, firm wine of extraordinary depth.

Heublein bought the vineyard from the de Latour family in 1969, and André Tchelistcheff retired four years later, but the present operation is in the very capable hands of Legh Knowles and Tom Selfridge. The high quality of vintages since Tchelistcheff's departure indicates a willingness on the part of present owners and employees to continue in his tradition.

1974		1980		1981		1982	
OPEN	NOW	OPEN	NOW	OPEN	NOW	OPEN	NOW
$38	$700	$180	$240	$190	$240	$200	$260

Château Montelena
(Napa)

wine: Napa Valley Cabernet Sauvignon   production: 25,000 cases

Montelena became famous overnight. In a 1976 blind tasting organized by Stephen Spurrier of the Academie du Vin, the 1973 Chardonnay defeated four well-known white Burgundies. What made the triumph all the more sweet was the nationality of the judges—all were French. Montelena has since acquired a corresponding reputation for their Cabernet Sauvignon, not only as a long-lived wine, but one that appreciates as well. Montelena's first winemaker, Mike Grgich, now has his own vineyard, but his former assistant, Bo Barrett, has proven himself a more than capable replacement.

1977		1980		1981		1982	
OPEN	NOW	OPEN	NOW	OPEN	NOW	OPEN	NOW
$180	$330	$160	$196	$140	$196	$130	$200

Heitz Wine Cellars
(Napa)

wine: Cabernet Sauvignon, Martha's Vineyard   production: 37,000 cases

I have a distinct memory of two Frenchmen entering my shop in the late seventies and asking about a eucalyptus-flavored Cabernet. They were seeking the 1974 Heitz Martha's Vineyard Cabernet Sauvignon. Even then the wine was expensive, almost $25 a bottle. They were shocked, but they bought it anyway. I think they were dumbfounded on two counts: that an American wine could cost so much and that it could taste so good.

Whenever I'm in Napa I try to pay a call on Joe Heitz. He has an informal, direct way of dealing with people that can be off-putting if you don't know him. Last April we met in his driveway—I was arriving and he was leaving. He slowed down enough to say hello and invite me to dinner at seven o'clock; then speeded up and drove on.

Heitz' reputation is based on his abilities as a master winemaker rather than a grower of fine grapes. His fame derives from the wines he blends from judiciously selected grapes from the fine vineyards of friends. His Martha's Vineyard Cabernet (after Martha May, a vineyard owner, not the island retreat off the coast of Massachusetts) has been called the Mouton of Napa, by no less a figure than Hugh Johnson. It regularly receives spectacular reviews from wine critics.

Dinner with the Heitz family provides a telling insight into Joe Heitz' attitude toward his wines. We tasted his fine Cabernets, but also sampled Grignolino and several rosés—he is as proud of his lesser wines as he is of his masterpieces.

Heitz releases his wine four or five years after the vintage and they can be relatively expensive even when they first appear on the market. Even so, few California red wines can provide you with the rock-bottom security of this man's efforts.

1974		1977	
OPEN	NOW	OPEN	NOW
$40	$800	$120	$320

Robert Mondavi Winery
(Napa)

wine: Napa Valley Reserve Cabernet Sauvignon and Opus I
production: 300,000 cases (at the Oakville winery)

Robert Mondavi is an enormously enthusiastic innovator and promoter of American wines; he is probably the premier spokesman for American wine. In the short space of twenty years he has proven that volume and quality are not necessarily mutually exclusive. The production figure of 300,000 cases represents the output of varietal wines from his Oakville facility. Another million cases of jug wines issue from the winery at Woodridge.

Mondavi has two wines worth considering as investments, the N.V. Reserve Cabernet and Opus I, a collaborative effort with Baron Philippe de Rothschild, of Mouton-Rothschild. Right out of the gate Opus I commands a price equaled by first-growth red Bordeaux—$600 a case; the Cabernet Reserve costs about a third as much (in February of 1986 the 1982 Reserve sold in New York as short futures—deliverable in October—for $220). Both wines have excellent aging potential.

Opus I will probably be considered the ultimate in expensive, esoteric California wines (which may enhance its investment value), competing with other Franco-American efforts like Dominus. Retailers of fine wines receive an elegant notification of their allotment of Opus 1 on heavyweight bond paper signed personally by Robert Mondavi; you're asked to verify and return the notice to the winery. Earlier in the book I mentioned Mondavi's genius in marketing his wines. American vineyards don't have the centuries of history which sometimes enhance a French wine's reputation, but sales pitches cast like invitations to the royal ball will do nicely in a pinch. The 1982 Reserve, on the other hand, is a dependable, available great Cabernet (whose price rises quickly).

1981 Opus 1		1982 Cabernet Reserve	
OPEN	NOW	OPEN (2/86)	NOW
$360	$560	$220	$250

#2 IGW

Jordan Vineyard and Winery
(Sonoma)

wine: Cabernet Sauvignon
production: 70,000 cases

Tom Jordan's first release, his 1976 Cabernet Sauvignon, was such an instant success that it caused more than one envious vigneron to remark that *anyone* can make a great wine if he's willing to spend a million dollars on the best fruit, latest technology and most talented winemakers. Certainly Jordan never intended to create an unobtrusive or inexpensive little winery. He ages his wine in Lafite's old barrels, and the vatting room is a marvel of space-age equipment. One of the lavish private apartments in the winery (there are three) has a set of double doors which give onto the vatting room; others have spectacular views overlooking Alexander Valley. Few luxury hotels can match the accommodations Tom Jordan provides his guests. Guest suites aside, Jordan is probably the most beautiful vineyard in the world.

Tom Jordan's strategy has been to make wines that established his name in the market; then, with his reputation secure, to concentrate on Cabernets with the staying power and potential for long development. Jordan wines now carry such prestige that investors pay ridiculous prices for his first releases, ignoring the fact that the wines have passed their prime. His new wines will undoubtedly fetch even higher resale values.

1976		1980		1982	
OPEN	NOW	OPEN	NOW	OPEN	NOW
$100	$800	$110	$260	$120	$190

Ridge Vineyards
(Santa Clara)

wine: Monte Bello Cabernet   production: 40,000 cases

Located high in the Santa Cruz Mountains, in Cupertino, south of San Francisco, Ridge Vineyards was founded by a group of scientists from the Stanford Research Institute in 1959. Almost from the beginning, Ridge has produced controversial—sometimes exciting—wines. Three specific facts come to mind when I think of Ridge: the reputation of their Zinfandels and Cabernets; their use of wild yeast strains; and their bottling of 1967 Cos d'Estournel, Montrose and Lynch-Bages.

According to Alexis Lichine, this latter practice became illegal after 1969, but previous to that, perhaps as a way of drawing attention to the winery, Ridge purchased the 1967 vintage of these wines *en primeur* (still in the barrel), bottling it themselves. The strategy was quite successful; I bought almost all of their Montrose and had quite a successful run with it in New York.

In the late sixties and early seventies Ridge was a renowned producer of Zinfandel, at the height of that varietal's popularity. Interest in Zin has since declined and wine lovers have shifted a greater share of their attention to the Monte Bello Cabernet, an exquisite wine designed to last a long time. Paul Draper, the winemaker and one of the vineyard partners, recently found himself the subject of national attention when he began submitting Cabernets for testing at the University of California's Magnetic Resonance Facility at Santa Cruz. Draper is hopeful of isolating the molecular composition of specific flavor constituents in great wines, thus enabling the vineyards to produce fine wines with greater consistency.

Even if Draper doesn't succeed, Ridge has an excellent track record for producing IGW.

1980		1981	
OPEN	NOW	OPEN	NOW
$160	$380	$180	$280

Chappellet Winery
(Napa)

wine: Napa Valley Cabernet Sauvignon   production: 27,500 cases

Donn Chappellet's winery is a vision of the future, what you would expect to find dotting Napa hillsides in the year 2100. The interior is as cavernous as a gymnasium, with fermenting tanks and equipment occupying the three corners of the triangular structure. On one visit I followed Donn up the ladder to his office which looks down on the work space—an aerie as suited for meditation as for office chores.

Chappellet Cabernets are uncompromisingly tough in their youth; hard, tannic wines built with endurance in mind. Considering that Chappellet started back in 1968, and what American tastes were like in those days, the decision to make wines with potential for long aging required a leap of faith—both in the ultimate maturation of Chappellet wines and in the taste of American consumers. Both gambles have paid off. Chappellet Cabernets consistently receive high marks for concentrated, intense flavors which take years to mature, but eventually reward as only long-aged wines will. I think the wines are presently undervalued as a result of Donn Chappellet's aversion to middlemen. Buy them now; wines of this quality and reputation can only go up.

1980		1981		1982	
OPEN	NOW	OPEN	NOW	OPEN	NOW
$96	$140	$100	$155	$110	$165

Mayacamas Vineyards
(Napa)

wine: Napa Valley Cabernet Sauvignon   production: 5,000 cases

One broiling summer day in 1976 Gloria and I were cruising around Napa Valley when we decided we couldn't take the 110-degree heat any longer. A drive up into the Mayacamas Mountains seemed to offer refreshment so we headed up the Lokoya Road, an unbelievably steep climb that led to (among other places) Mayacamas Vineyards.

If any establishment deserves the epithet of "mountain vineyard" then Mayacamas is it. It *feels* unbelievably high and the log-cabin building repudiates the high-fashion characteristics of other vineyards on the valley floor. In such a setting monster red wines seem appropriate.

Words like "hulking," "monster" and "huge" are often used to describe John Travers' boutique Cabernets. Quite candidly, these wines are a little too big for me, but they've outlasted some of their earliest critics who claimed the fruit would never survive over the time it would take for the tannin to break down, a distinct asset when you consider investment potential.

One drawback is the limited production of Mayacamas. The Cabernet can sometimes be difficult to find, but if you do stumble across a case, you might be wise to buy it.

1981 Napa Valley Cabernet
OPEN	NOW
$120	$198

Grgich Hills Cellars
(Napa)

wine: Napa Valley Chardonnay   production: 20,000 cases

Mike Grgich is an energetic fireball of a winemaker who paid his dues at Mondavi and Château Montelena before getting his own vineyard in 1977 (in partnership with Austin Hills, of Hills Brothers Coffee). He has an obsessive dedication to making first-rate white wines; after his triumph with the 1973 Montelena he's seemed incapable of making a poor Chardonnay. During a visit to his vineyard last year we tasted some of his older wines (he's only had the vineyard since 1977); his 1978 Napa Valley Chardonnay reminded me of Corton-Charlemagne, a wine for special occasions. To my taste, his wines offer a feminine, European alternative to the heavily oaked, musclebound Chardonnays that have become California's trademark. In addition, I expect that his wines will age well, last fifteen or twenty years, like some of its Burgundian counterparts.

1981

OPEN   NOW
$120 $360

Clos du Val
(Napa)

wine: Cabernet Sauvignon, Reserve   production: 45,000 cases

Bernard Portet, winemaker at Clos du Val, has wine in his blood—his father was cellarmaster at Lafite until 1974. Portet's work at Clos du Val has done much to legitimate varietal blending in California; Baron Philippe de Rothschild recently remarked that California will never make it until winemakers learn to blend. Misguided purists quite rightly wishing to distinguish between jug wines and the finer efforts of varietal winemakers have encouraged production of unblended wines. In so doing they have denied California vintners use of one of the most important tools of their European counterparts—the ability to adjust for seasonal and regional variation in varietal characteristics. If you've experienced a one hundred percent Cabernet, whose complex nose and palatal subtleties disappeared beneath an astringent finish, then you'll know about the limitations of unblended wines.

Portet's Cabernets, softened with Merlot, demonstrated to purists that blending may as easily be employed to produce elegant wines as it may inexpensive ones. Portet now buys grapes from the cooler Carneros region as well as using the fruit from Clos du Val proper.

From an investment standpoint, the best choice of Clos du Val wines is the Cabernet Reserve, simply because its firmer structure and tannic backbone give it a greater aging potential.

1977 Cabernet Reserve

OPEN	NOW
$140	$290

Freemark Abbey Winery
(Napa)

wine: Cabernet Bosché   production: 28,000 cases

I've always tried to buy wines as direct as possible from the vineyard. For many years I ignored Freemark Abbey wines because they were only available, at considerable markup, through a New York wholesaler. What changed my mind was a taste of the 1976 Cabernet Sauvignon from the Bosché vineyard. The taste was sublime.

Freemark Abbey was more a star in the early seventies, perhaps because not as many people were making great wines. Intuition tells me that the winery is ripe for an infusion of fresh blood, either in the form of newer and younger partners, or maybe just an increased willingness to put its wines before the public palate.

In either case, buy the Cabernet Bosché, an unqualified recommendation; the present price is reasonable and the wine will almost certainly climb.

1978		1980		1982	
OPEN	NOW	OPEN	NOW	OPEN	NOW
$100	$350	$90	$250	$140	$190

Sterling Vineyards
(Napa)

wine: Cabernet Sauvignon, Private Reserve   production: 75,000 cases

Sterling is now owned by Seagram's, part of a package deal from the Coca-Cola Company, that also netted Monterey Vineyard in California and Taylor Vineyards in New York. Sterling wines have always given me the impression of not quite living up to the potential suggested by the ultramodern architecture and winery equipment—or to their early reputation for producing Bordeaux-style wines. Make no mistake, Sterling wines are expensive, but unlike other wineries which charge premium prices for their wines, I never thought the quality of Sterling quite justified the extra expense.

What interests me about the wine now is that Seagram's has purchased the Los Carneros vineyard of Rene de Rosa, thus guaranteeing themselves a source of top-quality grapes. Most vineyards don't have anywhere near the equipment, financing, or prestige of Sterling. My feeling is that the entire combination will now come together, resulting in wines whose quality more than matches their expense. Keep an eye peeled for Sterling, beginning with the 1985 vintage.

1979 Cabernet Sauvignon, Private Reserve

OPEN	NOW
$180	$240

Far Niente Winery
(Napa)

wine: Chardonnay   production: 12,500 cases

Far Niente is one of the few wineries I've listed which concentrates on just two wines—Chardonnay and Cabernet Sauvignon. Founded in 1979, their wines have been well received by those who prefer Chardonnays in the big, buttery, oaky style now associated with California. In my experience, these big wines have the greatest chance of living a long time. The winemaker seems resolutely committed to maintaining this style of wine even though other wineries have begun shifting to a lighter-style Chardonnay more in keeping with white Burgundies, making it a good bet as an investment. In the future, Far Niente will make wine from their own grapes on vines now maturing.

1983		1984		1985	
OPEN	NOW	OPEN	NOW	OPEN	NOW
$120	$240	$108	$230	$116	$260

Château St. Jean
(Sonoma)

wines: Chardonnay, Robert Young Vineyard
       Johannisberg Riesling or Gewürztraminer, Selected Late Harvest,
       Robert Young or Belle Terre Vineyard
production: 120,000 cases

Suntory, the Japanese liquor giant, purchased St. Jean in 1984 for a reputed $40 million, an unbelievable price for a vineyard and winery, and testament to the abilities of W. Kenneth Sheffield and Robert and Edward Merzoian, founders of the operation.

St. Jean's success may be attributed to winemaker Dick Arrowwood's relentless experimentation with vineyard-exclusive white wines (like Joe Heitz' reds). In some years St. Jean has released up to nine different Chardonnays as well as a raft of assorted Rieslings, Fumé Blancs and Gewürztraminers, a staggering (or stupefying) variety of wine.

St. Jean produces big, fat, oaky Chardonnays that appreciate nicely, but to me the true gems of this winery are the Selected Late Harvest Wines, true American rivals to the Beerenauslese and Trockenbeeren-auslese of Germany. Sweet dessert wines like these are the only exception to my general prohibition against buying half-bottles as investments. Not only do the wines have a high rate of appreciation, they keep for a very long time as well.

1983 Johannisberg Riesling, SLH, Robert Young Vineyard

OPEN	NOW
$400	$499

1984 Chardonnay, Robert Young Vineyard

OPEN	NOW
$120	$184

Joseph Phelps Vineyards
(Napa)
wine: Johannisberg Riesling, Selected Late Harvest
production: 60,000 cases

Joseph Phelps got off on the right foot with his winery in the early seventies—he sought the advice of Joseph Heitz. Presumably, Heitz steered him correctly because the winery has made wonderful wines since their first release. Phelps' reputation derives from former wine-maker Walter Schug's skill with Chardonnay and German-style Rie-slings and Gewürztraminers, although now the vineyard produces high-quality Cabernet as well.

The Selected Late Harvest Riesling is a standard in the industry. I remember tasting the 1976 next to a Château d'Yquem of the same year and thinking that the Phelps was in no way inferior. Walter Schug has since left to found his own winery, although he still maintains a consulting relationship with the vineyard. Recent production seem to have suffered not at all, perhaps because his assistant, Craig Williams, was an able learner.

As an investment I'd certainly recommend the S.L.H. Riesling, although recent prices have struck me as a bit on the high side. Even so, the appreciation of good vintages seems to justify stiff opening prices.

1976		1983	
OPEN	NOW	OPEN	NOW
$285	$560	$450	$600

#3 IGW

The wines in this last group suffer from a lack of reputation or availability, which is why my endorsement of them is qualified. Most of them do not have a history of being traded, but something about their production attracts me—the reputation of an owner or winemaker, a critical success or bargain price way out of proportion to quality. Were the investment potential of these wines a direct function of their taste, all would be #1 IGW; they are superior in all senses save one—their novelty.

Rutherford Ranch
(Napa)

wine: Cabernet Sauvignon   production: 7,000 cases

Rutherford Ranch is actually a proprietary label for Round Hill Cellars. Rutherford Ranch wines are varietal wines usually made from single vineyards, selected each year by the Round Hill owner, Ernie Van Asperne. As exclusive New York distributor for the inexpensive varietals marketed under the Round Hill label, I came across the Rutherford Ranch wines several years ago. Van Asperen makes Pomerol-style blends of Cabernet and Merlot. The first release was only 200 cases of the 1976 vintage, a tough, chewy wine that took several years to harmonize. Today production has peaked at around 2,000 cases of the Cabernet, still structured to last. The 1982 and 1983 both taste raw, with enormous fruit and lots of tannin. Both of these should be exciting wines. Rutherford Ranch wines are too young to have a trading history; both vintages now (March, 1987) retail for $120 to $150 per case.

Chalone Vineyard
(Monterey)

wine: Pinot Noir   production: 12,000 cases

Of all the European grape varietals transplanted to California, Pinot Noir has been the least successful. Chardonnay and Cabernet wines from California have been made into wines which have equaled or bested their French competitors in blind tastings; the Pinot has not typically produced wines of similar caliber.

Enter Pinot Noir from Chalone Vineyard. Michael Michaud, the winemaker, quickly established the vineyard's reputation for Chardonnay; then in the late seventies he began producing Pinot Noirs that suggested Californians might learn to exploit the red grape of Burgundy after all. The only drawback to this phenomenon is the vineyard's limited production. Most of their output is devoted to white wines, and even those are not always readily available. If you come across Chalone's Pinot Noir, snap it up.

1982 Pinot Noir
OPEN   NOW
$110 $240

Dunn Vineyards
(Napa)

wine: Cabernet Sauvignon   production: 1,000 cases

This is the smallest-production vineyard listed in this book. Randy Dunn is the winemaker at Caymus Vineyards, but beginning with an outstanding 1979 vintage he began releasing Cabernets made from grapes on his own six-acre vineyard. His wines have received incredible reviews as complex, firm, tannic wines in the Bordeaux tradition. I also have to admit that clients of mine who frequently do business in California have talked up this wine ever since its appearance. Were it not for the sensational reviews I'd be tempted to dismiss the rumors as more cachet-as-catch-can.

1984 Cabernet
OPEN   NOW
$90 $180

Duckhorn Vineyards
(Napa County)

wine: Napa Valley Merlot   production: 10,000 cases

This place looks like a small private home on the corner of Lodi Lane. During my single, brief visit to the winery, I waited in their office while a woman attended to an incessantly ringing telephone, patiently repeating her explanation that they had no more wine available. Was I witnessing a charade performed for the benefit of visiting wine merchants?

In any event, Daniel and Margaret Duckhorn, and their winemaker Tom Rinaldi, produce fabulous Cabernets and a gutsy Merlot with much more substance that looks and tastes as though it were intended to last—if you can find it.

1983 Napa Valley Merlot
OPEN   NOW
$90 $180

Vichon Winery
(Napa)
wine: Napa Valley Cabernet Sauvignon, Fay Vineyard
production: 45,000 cases

Robert Mondavi inspires the same confidence in me regarding California ventures that Jean-Pierre Mouiex does with his French ones. Vichon began as a limited partnership of people in the restaurant and hotel trade in 1980. Several years later the venture was sold to Robert Mondavi. Under winemaker George Vierra (an old Mondavi hand) the vineyard is producing concentrated, medium-weight Cabernets designed to last.

1982 Napa Valley Cabernet Sauvignon, Fay Vineyard

OPEN	NOW
$80	$132

Sequoia Grove Vineyards
(Napa)
wine: Napa Valley Cabernet Sauvignon   production: 8,000 cases

This wine is a longshot that may prove profitable. The vineyard is presently in the hands of an immensely successful importer, the firm of Kobrand. Until recently the firm had no California wines at all (it turned down Jordan ten years ago). My guess is that Kobrand now wants to position itself in the market for California wines and will do it with Sequoia Grove. Since the wine is presently modestly priced, you may want to gamble on it. 1982 Napa Valley Cabernet Sauvignon is presently available for $130 a case.

Chimney Rock Vineyard
(Napa)
wine: Cabernet Sauvignon

Wine lovers on the prowl for future IGW could do a lot worse than Chimney Rock. The vineyard shares the same microclimate as its famous neighbors, Clos du Val and Stag's Leap. Hack Wilson and his wife, the owners of Chimney Rock, are presently growing Cabernet and Chardonnay, and making wines under the supervision of Mike Robbins, owner of Spring Mountain. Mrs. Wilson is a member of the DeBeers diamond family, at the very least a guarantee that the vineyard will have the financial resources to weather the difficult years of waiting while their vines mature. Their first Cabernet will be relased in 1987, probably for around $150 per case.

Dominus
(Napa)

wine: Cabernet Sauvignon

Dominus is Christian Mouiex's sally into California wine, in this case a partnership with the heirs of John Daniel (of Inglenook fame). The first release, the 1982 vintage, was supposed to appear on the market in the fall of 1986. Robert Parker, Jr., gave the wine a sensational review and collectors geared themselves up for a tasty, if expensive, treat. Mouiex decided to delay the release of the wine another year, however, perhaps deciding that it required an additional twelve months of bottle aging. The wine is now scheduled for release in late 1987, most probably for around $1,200 a case.

Considering Mouiex's reputation, the wine will almost certainly become a collector's item for those wealthy enough to afford it.

CHAPTER ELEVEN

PORT ET ALIA

A ny serious strategy of wine investing should include some consideration of Port. Without a doubt Port is the safest and most profitable liquid asset you can buy.

If it's so important, I can hear you asking, why haven't you devoted a chapter exclusively to it?

The answer's easy—there's almost nothing to explain. Buy True Vintage Port, then keep it until the price goes through the roof. If you think I'm joking, take a look at the rate of appreciation for the brands listed on the Port chart below. As a rule, prices for True Vintage Port move in common, with about a ten percent variation from brand to brand. Unlike the other types of wine described in this book, there's little esoterica to master, even for the enthusiast. The world of Port moves slowly, and the major houses have long, established histories, for

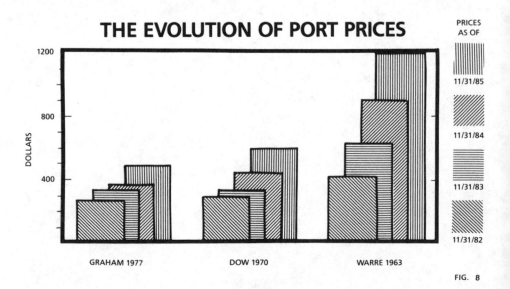

THE EVOLUTION OF PORT PRICES

PRICES AS OF

11/31/85

11/31/84

11/31/83

11/31/82

DOLLARS

1200

800

400

GRAHAM 1977   DOW 1970   WARRE 1963

FIG. 8

138

quality production and high resale value. Moreover, Port is the longest-lived #1 IGW of all.

Port's methuselan ability to age derives in part from the fact that it's a fortified wine. Makers of Port follow a different procedure than their cousins in Napa or Bordeaux; fermentation is allowed to proceed only partway and then grape brandy is added to the half-fermented grape juice. The high alcohol content of the mixture stops the fermentation. The resultant mixture is dark, sweet and highly alcoholic.

True Vintage Port, like Bordeaux wines, may be a blend of several different batches of wine, and also like Bordeaux, after blending it's transferred to oak casks, where it ages for two years before bottling. Other types of Port spend greater amounts of time in wood, depending on the desired character of the wine. Vintages are declared only in exceptional years, perhaps three times in a decade. Not all firms will declare a vintage in a given year; the collective sense about the value of a vintage may be measured by the number of firms that declare the vintage. Stay away from investing in Ports where the majority of firms do not declare vintages.

My good friend and Port expert Christopher Collins was kind enough to supply me with comments regarding vintage years:

1945 1948 1955	Excellent years. Wines from these vintages are mature but still characterized by that marvelous freshness and zest indicative of a lengthy future. Of these the 1945 is the greatest.
1960	Mature Port which is drinking well now, but not in the same class as the previous vintages.
1963	Outstanding vintage, the best since the 1945. Decanted well in advance, it can be tackled now, but ideally shouldn't be drunk until the late 1980s. It should last comfortably into the twenty-first century.
1966	Good for current drinking.
1970	Excellent vintage which will be good drinking in the next four or five years. Still a bargain despite recent increases in price.
1975	A lighter vintage, but a useful stopgap after drinkers exhaust the 1960s and 1966s (and the 1970 remains too young). Drinkable now. Also recommended by Michael Broadbent.
1977	A big long-haul vintage. No Port lover worth his salt will touch these bottles until the 1990s. A vintage no Port cellar should be without.
1980	Not a particularly important vintage and probably rather lightweight. Given the longevity of some of its predecessors, you could probably pass on this vintage with impunity.

1983 The equivalent of a 1961 Bordeaux, a marvelously rich wine, on a par with the 1963 Port vintage. Should be a superb investment.

The following firms represent the core of any Port investment strategy. I've commented on each of the firm's styles so you can match your own drinking preferences with the characteristics of an individual firm. But viewed as investments, all of them make worthy purchases.

Taylor. Same ownership as Fonseca. Owned by Robertson family and is generally highest-priced Port. Graham presents the only serious challenge to Taylor's auction supremacy.

	1963		1983	
OPEN	NOW	OPEN	NOW
$40	$750	$170	$275

Fonseca. Top of the line Port house. The 1983 was considered the wine of the vintage, an honor also claimed by the 1970.

	1977		1983	
OPEN	NOW	OPEN	NOW
$80	$750	$160	$399

Croft. Owned by the Gilbey's, familiar to Americans for their gin. Croft is a fine Port, although not quite up to the level of a Taylor or Graham.

	1963		1977	
OPEN	NOW	OPEN	NOW
$35	$900	$70	$390

Quinta do Noval. Owned by the independent Portuguese family, the Van Zellers. In very good years the estate makes about 1,000 cases of Nacional, the world's most expensive Port. Oddly, the firm did not declare a vintage in 1983, although they had declared in 1982, when most other estates had suffered a poor year.

	1970		1977	
OPEN	NOW	OPEN	NOW
$50	$475	$70	$450

Graham. Same ownership as Dow and Warre, although Graham is considered the leading wine. The 1970 Graham was considered (along with the Dow and Warre) a leader of the vintage. In terms of investment reliability, Graham is equaled only by Taylor.

1977		1983	
OPEN	NOW	OPEN	NOW
$75	$650	$165	$355

Warre. Owned by the Symington family. Reputedly made only 800 cases of the 1963, which is generally considered one of the best of that fabled year.

1963		1983	
OPEN	NOW	OPEN	NOW
$40	$1,200	$70	$600

Dow. Medium to good quality in average years, but capable of producing outstanding wines in great vintages (e.g., 1963 and 1983). Good value for your money in a great year.

1963		1983	
OPEN	NOW	OPEN	NOW
$34	$970	$125	$225

Sandeman. Owned by Seagram's. Big production of an accessible wine. Considered middle-of-the-road. The year 1927 was a truly great year and is still available.

1935		1977	
OPEN	NOW	OPEN	NOW
$16	$2,400	$65	$460

Cockburn. Currently the largest-selling True Vintage Port in England. Since London makes the market, this could be a sleeper.

1963		1983	
OPEN	NOW	OPEN	NOW
$35	$938	$125	$325

SWEET WINES

Sweet wines, specifically Sauternes and the best German wines, are God's way of providing an honorable occupation for obsessive-compulsive

vintners. Meticulousness is all. Nothing else in winemaking compares
to the labor-intensive effort necessary to give birth to a great d'Yquem
or a Wehlener-Sonnenuhr Trockenbeerenauslese, for instead of the ordinary grower's preoccupation with picking all of the fruit off his vines
in one fell swoop, the vigneron of sweet wines must harvest only grapes
of a precise degree of ripeness. Usually this means a minimum of three
or four passes through a vineyard, and sometimes as many as nine or
ten, and it also necessitates highly skilled pickers adept at recognizing
and picking individual ripe grapes, rather than whole bunches of fruit.
The extended time necessary for this type of harvest increases the risk
of a damaging rain or frost.

Although France makes dozens of sweet wines and Germany
hundreds, for investment purposes we need only consider a handful from
each country. For the moment, sweet wines are out of fashion; in an
auction catalogue of twenty pages, a page and half devoted to these
natural liqueurs is an unusually high representation. Also, while a consideration of their labor-intensive production makes sweet wines a good
value, they are almost never inexpensive, and the best of them command fabulously high prices.

Germany produces more sweet wine than any other country, but
the technicalities of a German wine label, the difficult pronunciation
of the wine names and the high cost has kept most of them from being
heavily traded. Sauternes are obscure, but the names are at least easily
mastered and all the wine of a given château's vineyard may be assumed
to be of the same quality. In Germany, as in Burgundy, a specific grower
within a general vineyard can mean the difference between greatness
and mediocrity.

Both German wines and Sauternes share one peculiar characteris-
tic: wines from the best years are made from grapes attacked by the
botrytis cinerea mold. Known as *pourriture noble* in French and *edelfäule*
in German, this mold causes the grapes to lose their moisture, concen-
trating the sugar and elevating the glycerin content. Regardless of the
type of grape involved, whether the Sémillon and Sauvignon Blanc of
Sauternes or the Riesling of Germany, wines made from botrytic grapes
have a distinctive apricot flavor instantly recognizable to connoisseurs
of late-harvest wines. The wines also have a high acid content which,
in tandem with their concentrated fruit, enables them to last much
longer than ordinary white wines. A thirty-year-old bottle of white Burgundy might still be good, but more likely than not you're buying a
wine that's over the hill; a late-harvest wine from the same year will
still be as vibrant and fresh as the autumn day on which the grapes
were harvested.

SAUTERNES

Château d'Yquem
(Sauternes)

production: 6,500 cases   Premier Grand Cru

This is the world's number one sweet wine, in good years an incredibly concentrated nectar redolent of honey, with prices to match. I first brought d'Yquem into my shop in 1965—we were selling the 1962, a great vintage. The price for a case was a heart-stopping $150, yet even then lovers of sweet wine scoffed it up in no time. Now it is $2,000 per case. Recently I came across a chance to buy fifty cases of the 1975 for the bargain price of $600 per case. Within one afternoon all fifty cases disappeared from my shop—at $750 each. Six months later the price was over $1,000.

D'Yquem is one of the few wines I've ever personally coveted. On first visiting the Florentine restaurant Enotecca Pinchiorra I was flabbergasted to discover a carpeted corridor with floor-to-ceiling racks containing magnums and double magnums of this wine. I made the owner an offer on the spot, which he cheerfully refused.

1967		1975		1979		1980	
OPEN	NOW	OPEN	NOW	OPEN	NOW	OPEN	NOW
$100	$2,400	$290	$1,000	390	$800	$360	$660

Château Guiraud
(Sauternes)

production: 11,000 cases   first-growth

A recent surge in price has made Guiraud attractive. The prices for this wine have almost doubled since the 1979 vintage. No doubt a recent infusion of Canadian money accounts for the price climb; new owners and fresh commitment to a costly enterprise are always encouraging signs in Sauternes. I've also noticed a scarcity of this wine in recent vintages that I haven't noticed in other Sauternes, possibly the result of the château's buying back wine.

1978		1979		1981		1983	
OPEN	NOW	OPEN	NOW	OPEN	NOW	OPEN	NOW
$120	$290	$135	$260	$160	$320	$180	$360

Château Coutet
(Barsac)

production: 6,500 cases   first-growth

Coutet gets my vote for elegance and finesse. Some Sauternes can be oppressively heavy; this wine manages to retain some of the virtues of a late-harvest wine in a lighter style. In particularly good vintages the wine is labeled "Cuvée Madame."

1979		1980		1981	
OPEN	NOW	OPEN	NOW	OPEN	NOW
$100	$290	$180	$260	$130	$190

Château Climens
(Barsac)

production: 6,000 cases   first-growth

Climens is another currently fashionable sweet wine. Again, like Coutet, it inclines toward lightness and finesse rather than the dense-liqueur consistency that dominates Sauternes. Prices on older vintages have appreciated nicely. At a recent auction I saw the 1961 knocked down for $500 a case and the 1976 go for $250. Present taste favors light wines; the lighter Sauternes are likely to be the most popular of the sweet wines. Trading activity around Coutet indicates that interest in it as an investment has already begun.

1978		1979		1981		1983	
OPEN	NOW	OPEN	NOW	OPEN	NOW	OPEN	NOW
$90	$240	$120	$210	$135	$200	$110	$375

Château Suduiraut
(Sauternes)

production: 10,000 cases   first-growth

Suduiraut is a wine that I selected as IGW exclusively on the basis of recent activity in older vintages—the 1967 is presently $700, if you can find any. Again, it's a lighter Sauternes, very much the antithesis of the d'Yquem style. Vintages since the 1978 seem undervalued to me.

1978		1979		1981		1983	
OPEN	NOW	OPEN	NOW	OPEN	NOW	OPEN	NOW
$80	$210	$96	$190	$115	$180	$135	$330

Château Rieussec
(Sauternes)

production: 9,000 cases

first-growth

Rieussec strikes me as considerably undervalued—look at the price of the 1961! Château Lafite bought Rieussec in 1983 and has started marketing a dry white wine called Château R (wine which practically walks out of my shop, as soon as clients discover it's owned by Lafite). My guess is that the estate is on the rebound. If so, these low prices won't last long.

1961		1975		1978		1983	
OPEN	NOW	OPEN	NOW	OPEN	NOW	OPEN	NOW
$25	$480	$40	$180	$55	$200	$135	$360

GERMAN WINES

I selected the following wines on the basis of their trading history and their recognition outside Germany. They differ from French sweet wines in their lower alcoholic content and in their sugar content. This is not the place to explore the subtleties of German wine classification, except to note that quality, from a German perspective, is often a measure of sweetness. Wines are graded according to their sugar content, a function, naturally enough, of the ripeness of the grapes at harvest; and in the case of very sweet wines, of the presence of the botrytis mold.

For investment purposes, you should only consider wines with ratings of "Spätlese" or above. The categories, in ascending order of sweetness (and lateness of harvest) are: Kabinett, Spätlese, Auslese, Beerenauslese and Trockenbeerenauslese. Eiswein is made from grapes which have remained on the vine until a late date, then frozen solid; the wine is very sweet, but unlike botrytic wines, may need years of aging to harmonize its constituent elements.

Wehlener Sonnenuhr
(Mosel)

Wehlen is a village located on the Middle Mosel. The vineyard, with its huge sundial (sonnenuhr), sits on a slope on the opposite side of the river. Make sure, if you decide to gamble on this light, sweet wine, to purchase the J. J. Prum bottling, your guarantee that you're getting wine from one of the best sections of the vineyard.

1979		1982		1983	
OPEN	NOW	OPEN	NOW	OPEN	NOW
$70	$160	$40	$96	$56	$140

Schloss Vollrads
(Rheingau)

Schloss Vollrads is unusual in that the entire vineyard is in the same hands (simplifying the task of buying a bottle). An elaborate system of colored capsules identifies the level of sweetness of each bottle. Since the best bottles are made in small quantities and the labels superficially resemble one another, take care to buy the gold capsule (Beerenauslese) or the gold capsule with two stripes (Trockenbeerenauslese).

Beerenauslese				Trockenbeerenauslese			
1982		1983		1982		1983	
OPEN	NOW	OPEN	NOW	OPEN	NOW	OPEN	NOW
$180	$380	$250	$450	$550	$700	$600	$800

Bernkasteler Doktor
(Mosel)

Bernkasteler Doktor may quite likely be the most famous German wine in the world, which has perhaps driven the price beyond the actual value of the wine. In any auction catalogue which lists German wine you'll find a vintage or two of the good Doktor looking for a buyer. The vineyard has two principal owners, the widow of Dr. Thanisch and the Deinhard firm. My own opinion is that the Thanisch is the superior of the two.

1980		1981		1983	
OPEN	NOW	OPEN	NOW	OPEN	NOW
$200	$280	$180	$240	$240	$360

CHAMPAGNE

Only mad dogs and Englishmen could love old champagne, yet bottles of the stuff persist in showing up in auction catalogues. I don't advise you to invest in champagne. An auctioneer once confided to me that he suspected every third bottle of champagne over twenty years old was a dud (which may explain the desultory appreciation in old vintages). Also, good champagne rarely sold at bargain prices, and I've *never* heard of the price of an old champagne vintage suddenly taking off, the way wine from Bordeaux or California is sometimes inclined to do.

Still, if you're feeling foolish, here's a brief schematic of your alternatives.

Dom Perignon

I suppose if there's a blue-chip of champagne, then Dom Perignon is it. The 1961 is currently $1,200 a case; the 1966 and 1969 $1,000 per case. Of late, wine writers have taken to debunking the story that Dom Perignon, cellarmaster at the Abbey of Hautvillers, invented champagne, but as Alexis Lichine points out, perhaps his most valuable contribution was the invention of the cork.

Whatever his contribution, the sparkling wine which bears his name has become synonymous with luxury. Moët et Chandon, which owns D.P., entertains guests in high style at their palatial country house. The night I happened to be there the French race-car team was also invited. One leaves with the feeling of having been fêted in the most indulgent manner possible—an appropriate image for Dom Perignon.

1971		1973		1975 (Rosé)		1978	
OPEN	NOW	OPEN	NOW	OPEN	NOW	OPEN	NOW
$80	$1,200	$110	$900	$460	$1,400	$300	$590

Krug

In 1983 I visited the house of Krug and was treated to one of the most self-reverential disquisitions of an estate's history that I'd ever heard. Despite my liking the taste of the champagne, I was glad I'd only allotted myself thirty minutes for the visit. Krug is a relative newcomer to the U.S.; their vintage champagne has only been marketed here for three years—and it will probably take another three or four for it to catch on. In England, where Krug is known and popular, old vintages command large sums. The champagne has a sturdiness about it that's lacking in wines with more finesse. I think it's built to last.

1970		1973		1975		1978	
OPEN	NOW	OPEN	NOW	OPEN	NOW	OPEN	NOW
$290	$525	$240	$600	$270	$560	$320	$660

Pol Roger

Just in case it slipped your mind that Winston Churchill consumed a bottle of Pol Roger every night, a painted likeness hangs inside the house to remind you. A Union Jack snapping briskly from the flagpole and winery employees garbed in crisp white lab coats lend a proper British cast to the whole operation (the owner is French). I happened to meet Mme. Roger in London in 1967. At the time she was about fifty and looked twenty years younger, definitely a glamorous match for her champagne.

The Vintage Brut is a prestige *cuvée*, and I think as fashion casts its fickle affection in new directions this may be the next candidate for the title of flashiest champagne around, a position currently held by Roederer Cristal.

1978		1979		1981	
OPEN	NOW	OPEN	NOW	OPEN	NOW
$120	$200	$120	$310	$180	$260

Roederer Cristal

Roederer Cristal has supplanted Dom Perignon in the hearts of rock-and-roll stars. The Cristal Rosé presently retails for around $1,500 per case, more than double the price of Dom Perignon! This is an instance of money and prestige chasing itself. Granted, the lovely peach color of the Cristal Rosé is a beautiful sight, but the extravagant price for this wine seems excessive even by the standards of champagne.

Don't buy it for investment until the price comes down. It would have to vault to truly astronomical levels for you to make any money.

1979		1979 (Rosé)		1981	
OPEN	NOW	OPEN	NOW	OPEN	NOW
$290	$640	$680	$1,400	$400	$690

Bollinger

Vintage Bollinger from the early sixties regularly sells for around $1,000 a case. I have a famous client who loves this champagne, but won't buy it in less than ten-case lots because (as he informed me) the estate raises their prices every eighteen months. In any event, Bollinger is a high-profile wine that's managed to elude negative connotations of flashiness often associated with other expensive champagnes.

1979		1981 (Rosé)	
OPEN	NOW	OPEN	NOW
$190	$340	$260	$380

ODDS AND ENDS OF INVESTMENT GRADE WINE

After examining the riches of Bordeaux, California and Oporto it's easy to forget that most of the world's vineyards do not produce IGW. The simple fact that a wine costs an arm and a leg, as I've drummed into you, is no guarantee that the wine has a shred of investment value. One or two IGW vineyards among hundreds of other fine wines is usually the best we can do for the majority of the wine-growing regions of the world.

The following vineyards are the exceptions, the vineyards whose history and quality have distinguished them from their neighbors. Years of study may be required to sift through the various vineyards and the ribbonlike parcels appointed to different growers in Burgundy, but everyone immediately recognizes Romanée-Conti. Gaja Barbaresco, Biondi-Santi, Brunello di Montalcino and Guigal Côte Rôtie are names that also ring familiar. All of these wines have established resale value.

Burgundy

Burgundy vineyards are modest by comparison to the grand estates of Bordeaux. In 1964 I made my first trip to Burgundy. Arriving at the Hôtel de la Poste in Beaune in the early evening I telephoned M. Aubert de Villaine, one of the principal owners of Domaine de la Romanée-Conti, and made an appointment to see the vineyard the next day.

The vineyard for the world's most expensive Burgundy has none of the elaborate trappings which would characterize the property were it situated in the Médoc. The stone buildings seem to disdain the ornamental fripperies of Bordeaux. Less secure of my wine knowledge than I am today, I attempted to impress the cellarmaster with my knowledge of vinification terms. His only response was to blink at me, as though baffled about why I went to so much intellectual effort over a process that was essentially intuitive.

Romanée-Conti

1978		1981		1982		1983	
OPEN	NOW	OPEN	NOW	OPEN	NOW	OPEN	NOW
$600	$2,000	$750	$1,650	$800	$1,900	$1,000	$1,600

La Tâche

1978		1979		1982		1983	
OPEN	NOW	OPEN	NOW	OPEN	NOW	OPEN	NOW
$450	$1,500	$490	$900	$620	$1,100	$690	$1,300

Richebourg
(Domaine de la Romanée-Conti)

1978		1979		1982		1983	
OPEN	NOW	OPEN	NOW	OPEN	NOW	OPEN	NOW
$470	$1,450	$510	$980	$660	$1,400	$690	$1,605

Romanée-St.-Vivant
(Domaine de la Romanée-Conti)

1978		1979		1982		1983	
OPEN	NOW	OPEN	NOW	OPEN	NOW	OPEN	NOW
$400	$860	$420	$820	$490	$960	$560	$860

Le Montrachet

Marquis de Laguiche:

1978		1979		1981		1983	
OPEN	NOW	OPEN	NOW	OPEN	NOW	OPEN	NOW
$400	$1,600	$520	$1,500	$690	$1,200	$720	$1,500

Domaine de la Romanée-Conti:

1978		1981		1983	
OPEN	NOW	OPEN	NOW	OPEN	NOW
$790	$5,000	$700	$4,200	$1,800	$3,000

Côtes Rôtie
(Rhone)

Côtes Rôtie is one of the few Rhône wines, along with Chateauneuf-du-Pape and Hermitage, which wine lovers consistently recognize and pursue. The name literally means "roasted slope" and refers to the sundrenched hillsides of the vineyard. While there are a host of growers associated with Côtes Rôtie, Guigal is the most consistent and flavorful. He blends several different *cuvées*. Both his regular Côtes Rôtie and the one labeled Côtes Brune et Blonde have the reputation and trading history to make them worthwhile investments.

Côtes Rôtie (regular bottling):

1978		1979		1981		1982	
OPEN	NOW	OPEN	NOW	OPEN	NOW	OPEN	NOW
$60	$300	$60	$240	$144	$360	$155	$375

Côtes Rôtie (Côtes Brune et Blonde):

1978		1979		1981		1982	
OPEN	NOW	OPEN	NOW	OPEN	NOW	OPEN	NOW
$84	$480	$72	$430	$204	$540	$214	$567

Barbaresco
(Italy)

Barbaresco is one of the two principal red wines of the Piedmont; the second is Barolo. Although both wines are made from the Nebbiolo grape, Barbaresco stands in relationship to Barolo in the way that many Burgundies compare to Bordeaux wines: in place of restraint, there's accessibility; in place of complexity, a single monochromatic wash of flavor; and in place of austerity, warmth. Both wines may be very long-lived.

Many good Barbarescos remain anonymous, unknown to any except the most devoted connoisseur of Italian wines. In the case of Angelo Gaja however, we have winemaking talent and marketing genius fused together. The Gaja family have put their wines on the tables of the world—and the result is that Gaja Barbaresco is now the benchmark by which all others are judged. Gaja wines regularly appear in auction catalogues; their sturdy character assures them a healthy resale. For investment consider either of two bottlings, the Costa Russi or the San Lorenzo.

Gaja Barbaresco, Costa Russi:

1982		1983	
OPEN	NOW	OPEN	NOW
$260	$560	$290	$600

Gaja Barbaresco, San Lorenzo:

1982		1983	
OPEN	NOW	OPEN	NOW
$290	$600	$310	$640

Brunello di Montalcino
(Biondi-Santi)

Wine lovers accustomed to the taste of the Sangiovese grape in Chianti are often astonished upon tasting its incarnation in Brunello di Montalcino. Italian law requires that Brunello age four years in oak casks, a treatment that no doubt contributes to the raw, leathery quality of the wine in its youth. A *riserva* must age for one additional year, although the final year need not be in barrels. Such wines, obviously designed for the long haul, may take a decade before the first chinks appear in their tannic armor.

Brunello was first developed by the Biondi-Santi family in Tuscany in the 1840s. Although there are now many producers of Brunello, none has acquired the legendary status of the Biondi-Santi's, or the prices, which equal those of Bordeaux first-growths. Frankly, I've never found the wine to be equal to its reputation. I include it because it's one of the few Italian wines to appear at auction. I definitely do not recommend its purchase as an investment.

1970		1971		1977	
OPEN	NOW	OPEN	NOW	OPEN	NOW
$700	$1,700	$450	$1,100	$400	$800

APPENDIX I

STATE GOVERNMENT OFFICES

Alabama A B C Board
P. O. Box 1511
Montgomery, AL 36192
(205) 271-3840

Alaska A B C Board
201 East Ninth Street
Anchorage, AK 99501
(907) 277-8638

Arizona Department of
Liquor Control
1645 West Jefferson
Phoenix, AZ 85007
(602) 255-5141

Arkansas Department of A B C
7th and Wolfe streets (Box CO-500)
Little Rock, AR 77201
(501) 371-1105

California Department of A B C
1901 Broadway
Sacramento, CA 95818
(916) 445-6811

Colorado Liquor
Enforcement Division
1375 Sherman Street #628
Denver, CO 80261
(303) 866-3741

Connecticut Liquor
Control Commission
State Office Bldg. #562
Hartford, CT 06115
(203) 566-5926

Delaware A B C Commission
820 North French Street
Wilmington, DE 19801
(302) 571-3200

District of Columbia
A B C Board
614 H Street NW #807
Washington, DC 20001
(202) 727-3096

Florida Division of
Alcoholic Beverages and Tobacco
Johns Bldg.
Tallahassee, FL, 32301
(904) 488-7891

Georgia Alcohol and
Tobacco Tax Division
401 Trinity-Washington
Atlanta, GA 30334
(404) 656-4015

Hawaii Liquor Commission
650 South King Street
Honolulu, HI 96813
(808) 523-4458

Idaho State Liquor Dispensary
P.O. Box 59
Boise, ID 83707
(208) 334-3264

Illinois Liquor
Control Commission
201 West Monroe Street
Springfield, IL 62704
(217) 782-2135

Indiana Alcohol and
Beverage Commission
911 State Office Bldg.
Indianapolis, IN 46204
(317) 232-2430

Iowa Beer & Liquor
Control Department
1918 SE Hulsizer Avenue
Ankeny, IA 50021
(515) 964-6800

Kansas A B C Division
700 Jackson—Jayhawk Tower
Topeka, KS 66603
(913) 296-3946

Kentucky A B C Board
123 Walnut Street
Frankfort, KY 40601
(502) 564-4850

Louisiana Office of A B C
P.O. Box 66404
Baton Rouge, LA 70896
(504) 925-4041

Maine Bureau of
Alcoholic Beverages
State House—Station 8
Augusta, ME 04333
(207) 289-3721

Maryland Alcohol and
Tobacco Tax Division
State Treasury Bldg. #310
Annapolis, MD 21401
(301) 269-3311

Massachusetts A B C Commission
100 Cambridge Street
Boston, MA 02202
(617) 727-3040

Michigan Liquor
Control Commission
7150 Harris Drive, Box 30005
Lansing, MI 48909
(517) 322-1355

Minnesota Liquor
Control Commission
480 Cedar Street—Hanover Bldg.
St. Paul, MN 55101
(612) 296-6212

Mississippi A B C Division
P.O. Box 10175
Jackson, MS 39206
(601) 359-1046

Missouri Division of
Liquor Control
P.O. Box 837
Jefferson City, MO 65102
(314) 751-2333

Montana Liquor
Control Division
P.O. Box 1712
Helena, MT 59601
(406) 449-2540

North Carolina
Board of A B C
P.O. Box 26687
Raleigh, NC 27611
(919) 779-0700

North Dakota State Treasurer
Liquor Control Division
State Capitol
Bismarck, ND 58505
(701) 224-2643

Nebraska Liquor
Control Commission
P.O. Box 95046
Lincoln, NE 68508
(402) 471-2571

Nevada Department of Taxation
1340 South Curry Capitol
Compound
Carson City, NV 89710
(702) 855-4892

New Hampshire State
Liquor Commission
Storrs Street, P.O. Box 503
Concord, NH 03301
(603) 271-3132

New Jersey Division of A B C
25 Market Street, #Cn-087
Trenton, NJ 08625
(609) 984-3230

New Mexico Department of A B C
49 South Old Santa Fe Trail
Santa Fe, NM 87501
(505) 827-7760

New York Division of A B C
250 Broadway
New York, NY 10007
(212) 587-4192

Ohio Department of
Liquor Control
2323 West Fifth Avenue
Columbus, OH 43204
(614) 466-2142

Oklahoma A B C Board
P.O. Box 53445
Oklahoma City, OK 73105
(405) 521-3484

Oregon Liquor
Control Commission
P.O. Box 22297
Portland, OR 97222
(503) 653-3017

Pennsylvania Liquor
Control Board
Capital and Forester Streets
Harrisburg, PA 17124
(717) 783-8250

Rhode Island
Business Regulation Department
110 North Main Street
Providence, RI 02903
(401) 277-2562

South Dakota
Department of Revenue
700 North Illinois—Kneip Bldg.
Pierre, SD 57501
(605) 773-3311

South Carolina A B C Commission
1205 Pendleton Street
Columbia, SC 29201
(803) 758-2165

Tennessee Alcoholic
Beverage Commission
226 Capitol Boulevard, #604
Nashville, TN 37219
(615) 741-1602

Texas Alcoholic
Beverages Commission
P.O. Box 13127 Capital Station
Austin, TX 78711
(512) 458-2500

Utah Alcoholic
Beverage Control
P.O. Box 30408
Salt Lake City, UT 84130
(801) 973-7770

Vermont Department of
Liquor Control
State Office Bldg.
Green Mountain Drive
Montpelier VT 05602
(802) 828-2345

Virginia Department of A B C
2901 Hermitage Road
Richmond, VA 23261
(804) 257-0605

Washington Liquor
Control Board
Capitol Plaza Bldg.
Olympia, WA 98504
(206) 753-6262

West Virginia A B C Commission
310 57th Street SE
Charleston, WV 25304
(304) 348-2481

Wisconsin Department of Revenue
125 Weber—Box 8933
Madison, WI 53708
(608) 266-1611

Wyoming Liquor Commission
1520 East Fifth Street
Cheyenne, WY 82002
(307) 777-7129

APPENDIX II

THE RULES OF STRATEGY

Rule Number One: *Stick to my lists of investment-grade wine.*

Rule Number Two: *Never buy on the basis of taste alone.*

Rule Number Three: *Buy good wine in good years.*

Rule Number Four: *Physically inspect your wine.*

Rule Number Five: *Know the wine's provenance before you buy.*

Rule Number Six: *Never buy wine from someone you don't trust.*

Rule Number Seven: *Buy cases and large bottles.*

Rule Number Eight: *Buy some futures.*

Rule Number Nine: *Keep a cellar log.*

Rule Number Ten: *Do your homework.*

Rule Number Eleven: *Diversify.*

Rule Number Twelve: *Buy different vintages.*

Rule Number Thirteen: *Think of your investments over the long term.*

Rule Number Fourteen: *Watch for market breaks.*

Rule Number Fifteen: *Don't buy in times of excessively high prices.*

THE FINAL RULE: *Your investments should pay for your drinking wines. Make it happen.*

BIBLIOGRAPHY

Blue, Anthony Dias. *American Wine, A Comprehensive Guide.* Garden City: Doubleday, 1985.

Blumberg, Robert S. and Hurst Hannum. *The Fine Wines of California.* 3rd ed. Garden City: Doubleday, 1984.

Coates, Clive. *Claret.* London: Century, 1982.

Dovaz, Michel. *Encyclopedia of the Great Wines of Bordeaux.* Julliard, 1981.

Faith, Nicholas. *The Winemasters.* New York: Harper and Row, 1978.

Féret, Édouard. *Bordeaux and Its Wines* . . . Ed. Claude Féret. 13th ed. Bordeaux: Éditions Féret et Fils, 1986.

Johnson, Hugh. *Hugh Johnson's Modern Encyclopedia of Wine.* New York: Simon and Schuster, 1983.

———. *The World Atlas of Wine.* 3rd ed. New York: Simon and Schuster, 1985.

Lichine, Alexis, et al. *Alexis Lichine's New Encyclopedia of Wines and Spirits.* 3rd ed. New York: Knopf, 1984.

Millau, Christian. *Dining in France.* New York: Stewart, Tabori and Chang, 1986.

Parker, Robert M., Jr. *Bordeaux.* New York: Simon and Schuster, 1985.

Penning-Rowsell, Edmund. *The Wines of Bordeaux.* 1969. 4th ed. London: Allen Lane/Penguin, 1979.

Peppercorn, David. *Bordeaux.* London: Faber and Faber, 1982.

Rosengarten, David. "Modern Bordeaux." *The Wine Spectator.* 15 Nov. 1986: 28–29.

Spurrier, Steven and Michel Dovaz. *Académie du Vin Complete Wine Course.* New York: G. P. Putnam's; Christie's Wine, 1983.

INDEX